FLASHBA

The Flashback series is sponsored by the
European Ethnological Research Centre,
c/o the Royal Museums of Scotland,
Chambers Street, Edinburgh EH1 1JF.

General Editor: Alexander Fenton

Alan Harding

4.3.2002

Other titles in the Flashback series include:

THOMAS NELSON AND SONS

Memories of an
Edinburgh Publishing House

edited by
Heather Holmes
and David Finkelstein

TUCKWELL PRESS
in association with
SAPPHIRE: Scottish Archive of Print and
Publishing History Records
and
The European Ethnological Research Centre

The publisher and editors wish to thank Nelson Thornes for
its kind financial assistance in the publication of this volume.

First published in Great Britain in 2001 by
Tuckwell Press
The Mill House
Phantassie
East Linton
East Lothian EH40 3DG
Scotland

ISBN 1 86232 187 6

British Library Cataloguing in Publication Data
A catalogue record for this book is available
on request from the British Library

Typeset by Hewer Text Ltd, Edinburgh
Printed and bound by
Bell and Bain Ltd, Glasgow

CONTENTS

ILLUSTRATIONS

PREFACE

The occupational structure of Edinburgh has been described in its oral history. In the popular lore of the mid-twentieth century, one saying notes that 'Edinburgh is known for the three B's: Beer, Biscuits and Books'. Even though the printing and publishing industry employed a work force of between 5,000 and 7,000 people in the city well into the 1960s, little attention has been given to it or its importance. This is also true for the industry at a national level, where there are great gaps in the knowledge of it and its economic, social and cultural impact. For the twentieth century, a period of great change in the industry, there are few written autobiographies, histories of firms, or oral histories of the men and women employed in it.

This book results from the work of SAPPHIRE (Scottish Archive of Print and Publishing History), a major initiative established in 1998 to address the gap in the knowledge of the Scottish printing and publishing industries in the twentieth century. SAPPHIRE is a collaborative partnership between Napier University and Queen Margaret University College to preserve material on the social, economic and cultural history of these industries. It is presently creating a permanent oral and social history archive of the industry. It is utilising its gathered material to publicise and remind others of the cultural, social and economic significance of publishing and printing in Scotland's heritage. SAPPHIRE has been initiated and developed in collaboration with a number of individuals and organisations with experience in the printing

and publishing industry, oral history and heritage preserva-
tion, including the City of Edinburgh Museums, School of
Scottish Studies (University of Edinburgh), Strathclyde University, University of Aberdeen and the Scottish Publishers'
Association.

This book presents some of the collection work undertaken
by SAPPHIRE. At the point the project began in October 1998,
Thomas Nelson and Sons, one of the major publishing firms
in the city, would have celebrated its 200th anniversary. To
commemorate this event, a reunion was held with some of its
ex-employees at Abden House in Edinburgh, one of the
former homes of the Nelson family. At that meeting it became
evident that there was a great deal of oral tradition and lore
on the work, work culture, social history and history of the
firm which was not recorded in any of its surviving archival
papers. Follow-up interviews were carried out with these
employees and further calls were made to locate other Nelson
staff. Two more reunions were held and brought more
workers together.

This volume is a compilation of the testimonies of four ex-
Nelson employees who tell of their experiences in Nelsons
between the 1930s and 1968 when the printing side of the firm
was taken over by Morrison and Gibb of Tanfield, Edinburgh; one also recounts his working life after the takeover
and what happened to Nelsons after its Parkside Works
ceased production. They speak of work in a number of
departments throughout the firm, from administration and
office work through to production, and aspects of book
production. They relate how they obtained work in Nelsons
and learned their trade. They describe aspects of their work,
from the skills they learned as apprentices and journeymen, to
production techniques. They discuss their relationships in the
firm with co-workers, managers, management and other
departments. Through these, they show how workers and
the different trades viewed one another. Observations on

Preface

these relationships are especially important when it is considered just how central unions were to the industry during the period which is covered by their oral testimony. They make clear that Nelsons was not just a place of work but was also a social institution. The firm provided a range of social and welfare facilities for its workers, including an institute and bowling club. Some of its social activities, such as the organised dance at Christmas and the annual trip, were common also in other printing establishments and industries. The firm had a strong social fabric. As one informant noted, 'marriages were made in Nelsons'. Such a statement indicates the essence of the social fabric of Nelsons: a close-knit, family-run firm.

The interviews were selected to show the wide range of work and social cultures found in Nelsons. They highlight the uniqueness of the work of various departments, but also its commonality. Such themes are also extended into the arena of the social organisation. They provide a detailed record of the headquarters of one of Edinburgh's foremost publishers at a time of great change in the industry before it was altered completely by large-scale takeovers, mergers and the eventual demise of the industry. They also record part of the life and activity of the South Side community which surrounded the Parkside Works, a way of life that has now all but disappeared.

Heather Holmes and David Finkelstein

Acknowledgements

Funding from the following organisations has helped support the SAPPHIRE project in general, and the making of this volume in particular. These include grants from: the Carnegie Trust for the Universities of Scotland, the Gordon Fraser Charitable Trust, the Edward Clark Fund, the Edinburgh Booksellers Society, the Glenfiddich Living Scotland Award from John Grant Distilleries, and Nelson Thornes.

We would like to thank Helen Clark of the People's Story Museum and Jim Keppie for suggesting Thomas Nelson and Sons as an area of oral history research for SAPPHIRE; the Museum of Edinburgh for use of one of their photographs; John McDonald and Gordon Payne for use of their photographs; and Nelson Thornes for use of photographic material.

We would also like to thank: John Gunn, Bob Sinclair, Eric Martin and Bill Reid for telling their experiences; all the other former Nelson informants who assisted in the Thomas Nelson project of SAPPHIRE and who helped to shape our thoughts on the volume; also, Bill Styles, Napier University, for preparing the photographic material.

Finally, we would like to thank both Alexander Fenton at the European Ethnological Research Centre and Tuckwell Press for taking on this volume.

INTRODUCTION

A visitor to Edinburgh in 1914 looking westwards from the top of Arthur's Seat would have been struck by the noise and bustle emerging from the works of Thomas Nelson and Sons situated just outside the entrance to Holyrood Park. The constant clattering of the presses would have risen upwards to any spectator, while their eyes would have been drawn down to the constant coming and going at the plant as paper and other supplies were delivered and books in large quantities were dispatched to all parts of the world. Nelsons was at that time one of the most successful publishing houses in the world and its distribution network connected its Edinburgh headquarters to most English-speaking countries and much of Europe. The company had been trading in Edinburgh since 1798 when Thomas Nelson established a second-hand bookshop in a small, half-timbered shop with its counter opening on to the street at the head of the West Bow, near St Giles' Cathedral. (Its picture later acted as the colophon of Nelsons for many years.)

That experience as a bookseller convinced Thomas of the existence of a ready market for cheap, standard editions of non-copyright works, and he attempted to satisfy it initially by publishing in monthly parts well-known religious texts such as *Pilgrim's Progress* and *Scots Worthies* and then by issuing what became the Nelsons hallmark, popular reprints of classics such as *Robinson Crusoe* and *The Vicar of Wakefield*. The characteristics of the 'Nelsons formula' – low-price, outward-looking marketing, and a concern to promote the best of writing to a mass readership were apparent even at this early date. The books had to be inexpensive to be accessible to a new reading public of the skilled working classes, and Nelson employed the still uncommon process of stereotyping, invented by William Ged, another Edinburgh man, to reduce production costs over a large print run. In order to circumvent the hostility of a booktrade that saw its profit margins reduced, alternative outlets had to be found, for example through direct sales at fairs, at markets, or in vacant shops temporarily rented for the purpose. The Nelsons list expanded until in 1829 Thomas took the unprecedented step of employing a 'bagman', the first publisher's representative, to hawk his books around Scotland and the North of England. Not only was the firm commercially prosperous, but that prosperity accommodated the motivation to spread learning and knowledge through provision of good, cheap books, to promote 'the democratic intellect' through successful publishing.

The company gained its 'Sons' when William and Thomas entered their father's business in 1835 and 1839 respectively. Thomas, the father, died in 1861, after a period of invalidity, by which time he had abdicated total responsibility to his sons and they had established the running of the enterprise in their own way. William concentrated his talents on the marketing side, while Thomas devoted his to editing and production. In his early days with the firm, William attempted to reduce stock holdings by rebinding some of the reprints in a more attractive cloth finish and took to the road to sell them. The repackaging was successful, particularly coupled with an increased discount, and the booksellers who had earlier perhaps turned up their noses at the Nelson list now subscribed eagerly. In 1850 Thomas perfected a rotary press, a model of which was demonstrated at the Great Exhibition in the following year, but because Thomas had refused to patent his invention, little fame and no fortune resulted from the many clones which competitors built. A continuous web of paper fed cylinders holding curved stereotype plates passing the printed paper under a serrated knife for cutting into sheets. It is no exaggeration to state that this machine was the parent of all newspaper presses until well into the twentieth century. Each brother lent fresh energy and a natural acumen for publishing to the expansion of the firm although it still dealt only in reprints.

However, with the building in 1845 of a new printing house at Hope Park in Edinburgh, where the complete book-manufacturing process was eventually carried out under one roof, with a payroll of over four hundred employees, Thomas Nelson and Sons (in 1858 the company adopted its best-known title) began to initiate publication of stories of adventure and travel for young people, 'moral books', as well as educational titles generally. The former were to be especially suited to donation as Sunday school and church, or indeed weekday school, prizes to children, that is, reward books: their contents were elevating and wholesome; the books were attractively presented in accordance with the brothers' high standards; their price did not strain the purses of church committees or school boards. The work of R. M. Ballantyne, whose *The Young Fur-Traders*, published in 1856, was written at the suggestion of William Nelson out of Ballantyne's own experiences with the Hudson Bay Company, and was the first of seven major titles including *Coral Island* (1858) published by Nelsons before Ballantyne decamped to another house in protest over terms, fitted well into the category of 'moral books'. Harriet Beecher Stowe, an outstanding example of the moral, humane Nelsons author, was also among the more prominent writers, while artists such as Landseer and David Scott were numbered among the illustrators.

The various Education Acts after 1870 stimulated a tremendous demand for learning materials and Nelsons responded with the 'Royal Readers' series which sold in vast quantities throughout the British Empire. The Royal Readers were followed by the 'Royal School' series which eventually included some seventy titles. A watching brief was kept conscientiously on the market: the company corresponded with educationalists; it maintained contacts with school boards, at home and abroad, seeking always to answer particular needs; and the products of rivals such as Blackie and Arnold were monitored. Between 1878 and 1881 educational titles represented 25 per cent of the total output of Nelsons but yielded 88 per cent of the company's total profit. The Royal Readers themselves represented some 45 per cent of that total profit. Nelsons introduced the first school atlases, and Thomas is credited with the introduction into these of lines of latitude and longitude, and also of the scale in English miles. (He bought a controlling interest in John Bartholomew and Company, the cartographical and geographical specialists, not long before his death.) From these precedents, books on all subjects flowed from the Nelson presses to satisfy the need for good, cheap educational material. The *Highroads of History* (1907), the *Highroads of Literature* and the *Highroads of Geography* (both 1911) were to remain on the company's backlist for over forty years. Nelsons was also active in the periodical field. From 1895 *The Practical Teacher* appeared under its imprint. This, like many of the other periodicals issued, carried a high proportion of advertising for titles published by Nelsons and may have been regarded at least in part as a promotional medium for the firm. The most successful of the periodicals was *The Children's Paper* which Nelsons issued from 1855 until 1925.

A fire devastated Hope Park in 1878, causing damage estimated at between £100,000 and £200,000, only some of which was covered by the insurance on the buildings. Within two months Thomas Nelson and Sons were back in operation, albeit on a limited scale. Within two years the production works moved to the new site near Arthur's Seat. The calamity had brought the fortuitous benefit of investment in new plant from which a flood of reprints, school books, prize books and religious books poured — all at inexpensive prices. This was the site upon which our visitor would have gazed; that prodigious output would have accounted for the din and stir below. Efficiency had been gained not only through introduction of the latest technology but also through standardisation of the product. The books were grouped into various popular libraries, all to a standard size of 6.5 x 4.25 inches, such as the New Century Library which included titles by Dickens, Thackeray and Scott, 'handy for the pocket or knapsack, and especially suitable for railway reading'. The Sixpenny Classics, later just Nelsons Classics, began in 1903 as a reprint series of non-copyright works and was eventually to consist of over 400 volumes; the Nelson Library, selling at sevenpence, offered from 1907 reprints of copyright works in still familiar — at least to denizens of second-hand bookshops — red and gold cloth bindings. New titles were issued each fortnight and John Buchan, a recent addition to the firm, brought into the Classics fold works by James, Conrad and Wells. A Shilling Library provided a series of further copyright titles of general literature while several foreign series catered for languages other than English. A new factory was built in 1907 to undertake these and other series, capable of producing 200,000 books a week. The disinterested spectator would have agreed with John Buchan who wrote in retrospect in *Memory Hold-the-Door* (1940), his autobiography, of that pre-1918 period in the firm's history:

We were a progressive concern, and in our standardised Edinburgh factories we began the publication of cheap books in many tongues. On the eve of the war we must have been

Thomas Nelson and Sons

one of the largest businesses of the kind in the world, issuing cheap editions of every kind of literature not only in English, but in French, German, Magyar and Spanish, and being about to start in Russian.

However, the corollary of low prices is low profit margins and a dependence on maintaining high-volume sales. From 1878 to 1881 fiction represented 40 per cent of the total books produced but only 10 per cent of the total profit made by the firm over the same period. Furthermore, books by certain authors such as Ballantyne were much more profitable than the norm; 53 per cent of the profit from fiction was derived from 17 per cent of the titles. The conclusion must be that the greater proportion of the fiction published by Nelsons, including reprints, many of which were out of copyright, made very little money. Any contraction in constant volume sales would represent a threat to the company's continuing health. The First World War itself, through the denial of foreign markets, the loss of manpower and the general exigencies of wartime, led to the temporary rundown of Nelsons and initiated its long-term decline. Much of the effort expended during the inter-war period, particularly in expanding the education list and reducing the dependence on reprints, represented merely an attempt to reverse that decline.

After the death of Thomas Nelson III in 1917, Ian Nelson, his brother, took over as head of the family firm. The takeover of the publishing house of T. C. & E. C. Jack in 1915, with its strengths in children's titles, had consolidated the direction to which the company was to commit itself. Buchan brought in Sir Henry Newbolt, with whom he had worked in the Ministry of Information during the war, to act as editorial advisor in the educational field. Various series along the lines of its reprints were produced such as the Nelson 'School Classics'. In part response to Newbolt's own 1921 report on the teaching of English in schools in England

and Wales, Nelsons produced in 1922 'The Teaching of English' series (eventually running to some 200 titles) under the editorship of Newbolt himself and Richard Wilson. The latter also introduced a new type of school reader in *Reading for Action* and *Read and Remember*. A further series, 'The Teaching of History', also grew out of Buchan and Newbolt's collaboration. Indeed, Buchan's influence was apparent long after his leaving in 1929. (Ian Nelson remained head of the firm until his death in 1958.)

In the post-1945 period, this strategy was predominant: the education list became all-important to the company; and the tradition of cheap reprints, alive since its foundation, died. To compensate, overseas markets for textbooks were nurtured. The links Nelsons had had with the old Empire were reinforced in the new Commonwealth, especially in East and West Africa and the West Indies. In 1949 the Canadian branch became an independent company; in 1960 the Australian firm was established; in 1962 the South African branch was registered as a distinct company; a Nigerian company was set up in 1961; a Kenyan company followed in 1963: the development of Nelsons paralleled Britain's own movement from centre of Empire to member of Commonwealth. Even in 1887, a Royal Reader had been produced in the Nyanja language of what was then Nyasaland, now Malawi, and, sixty years on, Nelsons was publishing a wide range of textbooks in Kiswahili, Yoruba, Ewe, Twi and Ga. Specialist schoolbooks such as *West Indian Histories* and *Malayan Arithmetics* illustrated the company's determination to retain its hold on an important but vulnerable market.

Ian Nelson's successor, his son, Ronnie Nelson, seemed less interested in the successful management of the family firm than previous generations. In 1962 Thomas Nelson and Sons was absorbed into the Thomson Organisation in an effort to sustain its academic and educational publishing interests on a global scale. In common with other publishing enterprises at the time, the production plant was divorced from the publishing division. The former remained in Edinburgh, while the latter took up permanent residence in London. The publishers began to seek and accept competitive quotations for production work from a variety of printers in Britain and more frequently abroad. The printing division of Nelsons was sold to the Edinburgh company Morrison and Gibb in 1968; the Parkside Works, at one time the glory of the firm, were razed to the ground to make way for the headquarters of an insurance company. A visitor to Edinburgh today looking westwards from the top of Arthur's Seat would see only the reflected calm of the smoked-glass windows of the Scottish Widows building or the gleam of its near neighbour the Royal Commonwealth Pool; the only noise and activity would come from the constant flow of cars in and out of Holyrood Park. Perhaps this book and the voices captured within it will give to its reader some sense of the dynamism within Nelsons, its importance in the economic and social life of Edinburgh, all too apparent in the twentieth century but now part of its history.

Alistair McCleery,
Edinburgh, April 2001

Biographies

John Gunn

John Gunn was born in Edinburgh in 1919. He was educated at Sciennes Primary School from 1924 to 1929 and George Heriots from 1929 to 1936. He started work in Thomas Nelson and Sons on 5 April 1936 as a junior clerk in the counting room. Apart from a period in the armed forces (1940–46), he remained in that department until February 1950 when he moved to the 1/c sheet and bound stock. In 1957 he relocated to the London office where he was first the Warehouse Manager and then, from 1963, the Manager. In 1967 he left the firm to work as a Fees Accountant at the Girls' Public Day School Trust, Queen Anne's Gate, London. He retired in 1984 and currently lives in Edinburgh.

Eric Martin

Eric Martin was born in Edinburgh in 1928. He attended James Gillespies and then Boroughmuir School, before entering the printing trade in 1943. His apprenticeship was undertaken at Hislop and Day of Albany Street. He was employed in that firm, excluding a three-year period on National Service, until 1952. He then joined Thomas Nelson and Sons where he worked in the camera department until 1963, when he moved to the printing down department. After the firm closed, he spent a short period in Morrison and

Gibb, before moving to Waddie and Co. of Slateford Road in 1970. He remained there until 1992.

Bob Sinclair

Robert S. M. Sinclair was born in Edinburgh in 1939. He attended Moray House Demonstration School from 1944 to 1954. In August 1954 he entered Thomas Nelson and Sons. After a few months as an office messenger he started his apprenticeship in the caseroom, where he continued to be employed until 1961. He subsequently worked in a wide range of positions across the printing and publishing industry in Eastern and Central Scotland. This included work as Order Clerk in R. R. Clark Ltd (1961–66), as Estimator in George Waterston and Son Ltd (1966–67), and as Print Buyer/Sales Promotion Executive at Oliver and Boyd Ltd (1967–73). He was also employed in sales management and as a General Manager. More recently his work has been in the public sector at Lothian Regional Council and West Lothian Council. He is currently Printing Manager of Falkirk Council Printworks.

Bill Reid

Bill Reid was born in Edinburgh in 1934. He attended Milton House Primary School between 1939 and 1946 and James Clark Junior Secondary from 1946 to 1949. After leaving school he entered Thomas Nelson and Sons where he worked in the front office. After a few months he started his apprenticeship in the machine room. For a short time he also worked in the process laboratory. After leaving the firm in 1960, he was employed in sales and marketing for Aberdeen Paper Mill. From 1990 to 1996 he set up and established his own business, producing flexible packaging materials. He is now retired.

JOHN GUNN

1935. I was at Heriots and I was getting restless about what I was going to do, and I don't know who told me about the possibility of a vacancy in the counting room, which in effect was all the cash and accounts and that. And I went up and was interviewed by Archie, well Mr Cowan as I knew him then, Archibald Cowan. So he was the cashier, and he interviewed me and I probably got in very easily, in as much as apart from being asked to do some maths, I was also asked to do French. Unfortunately, I was taking German, not French. So he said, well, could I either say something in German, or write something for him, but nobody knew much German, so he decided I was quite a good prospect to come in and work. So on the basis of that, I started in Nelsons!

And, so, the next hurdle I had to face was a dear old lady, long since dead, and she was Miss Crawford. And she was really like a Victorian lady. She had the high black collars, and the black blouse and long skirt. And she said to me, when I was introduced to her, 'And what's your name?' And I said, 'John Gunn, but I'm called Jack'. And she said, 'Not in here you're not going to be Jack. You will be John, and you will call all the other members of the accounting staff Mr or Miss.' Oh but, as I was the junior, I was called John. So that was my introduction, then.

And so, amongst my jobs initially was taking the cheques to the bank, which was then in George Street, next to where St Andrew's and St George's churches, almost opposite the Dome, are now. Anyway, I had to take the cheques down

I

there and pay them in, and then on a Friday I had to go down with the man who was on the door as a sort of doorkeeper, who was a Mr Burns. And he had a great big, it was like a sheepdog. And every Friday we had a taxi, and he, who was about five foot four, and I mean I was six foot, and the dog, went down in the taxi to collect all the money for the wages for the factory. And of course in those days nobody attacked people, but it was just as well because the dog was the most docile animal ever! And he used to just lie there in the hall at the main entrance and never ever opened his mouth even to anyone walking in. So that was part of my early job. But eventually I was in the Counting Room. I was there until I went away to the army at the beginning o' 1940.

We had to, as part of the jobs, we also of course had to balance the ledgers. We had two book-keeping machines, two ladies on them, who recorded all the sales, and in addition, next door in the general office, there's a wages department and they, every Wednesday, collected all the work cards from the various departments and calculated the wages for each person. And they then sent them through to us in the counting room and we had to calculate the actual amount of pound notes, ten shilling notes, and silver and that for each department and then assemble all the various departments' wages into a grand total and then it went to the bank. That was the cash, and that happened of course every week. And in addition, monthly, we had all the sales ledgers and the girls created invoices which again went out at the end of the month, to customers. And then for overseas customers, there was inland bills, which were sent to customers for payment. And we also had to prepare all these figures for George Graham, who was then the main director.

I went to Heriot-Watt and had economics and commerce and I was really, not direct training but it was just word of mouth training from Mr Cowan, John Aitchison, who was the senior male, and Miss Crawford,[1] and the two ladies on

2

the book-keeping machines. That was the set-up there, then. Immediately next, we had what was called the export department, who had John Duncan, who was in charge, and Jessie Ross. The Rosses had a great association with Nelsons. They seemed to have sisters and sons, fathers, you name it. And they did all the export trade, as regards the books to be sent to our Canadian house or our agents in Australia and South Africa, and so they did their own side of the sales there. And that was the set-up, then we had the invoice typists generally in the general office. Ah, we had the Power Samus department. That was all card, card.

They had Burrows machines for the girls who did the statements and the invoices and they were very old. I mean we, even next door in the general office we had Burrows adding machines which were like countometers really — Oh you had to pull the handle on them. I mean they also, they could be used on, off, off electricity but it was never satisfactory though, I don't think.

We used to work Saturdays till twelve o'clock. When I started the works only had a week's holiday, in the summer. And we got two weeks, in the office, and we worked on Saturday. But the funny thing was when I started, there was a chap named Smith who was retiring and I was taking his place, and confidentially one day he said to me, 'Make sure you get taken on the permanent staff.' I said, 'Hmm?' I said, 'What's different to what I am just now?' He says, 'I, when I came back from the First World War,' he said, 'I was taken on in a temporary capacity,' and he says, 'That's never been changed and I've really been a temporary all these years.' And this was from the, after the war, the First World War, to 1935. So he said to me, 'Be sure you get taken on the permanent staff.'

I mean then, specially in the early days when I was working, it was quite difficult to get a job. Because at that time too there was an awful lot of, specially nearer the war, there was a lot of unemployment and the government of the day, I can't remember who was in power, but they set up an awful lot of schemes to teach unemployed, like bricklaying and joinery and things like that, to try and get them work, you know.

But the general office was really the biggest gathering of staff in the place and it was predominantly female. They mibby didn't replace some of the girls or something like that. It was that or pay off people, I mean that's the choice you have which is not happy, and although it didn't happen often, it did happen and I think they probably arranged it to stagger it so that if you were off one week, you wouldn't be off the next week. Somebody would be, another department would be off. But I don't say it happened all over, it would have only been certain departments who would have been affected by the fact that work wasn't coming forward for them. It would be short term. Well it must have been when I joined them in '35 and the outbreak of war, '39, somewhere probably between '35 and '37 I would have thought. It is a long time ago.

Ian Nelson was there.[2] He was, he was really the chairman, but he was there almost constantly. But he didn't take a direct interest in it. He was a very gentle gentleman, and spoke to everyone, but he didn't actually have a hands-on job at all. But George Graham, he was a real firebrand, and he used to shake people up periodically. So that was the sort of main thing. It was clerical, purely clerical, that I was involved in.

And then the Company Secretary, who was a Maurice Harding — long deceased — showed you how quiet things must have been then. He used to live in Falkirk and he used to travel through every day. But in the summer he had a place at North Berwick and he'd travel up. And this, this was every day! And he, well, he was always to me an old man, you know, but he did that every day in life and he was, until he retired, he was the Company Secretary.

4

We had a lady who, she had many hats. Miss Park — she used to be in charge of the canteen. You know where the canteen is in Nelsons? The building opposite the traffic lights as you come out the park. It's nice little flats now. But she was in charge of the canteen, that was one of her jobs. And then, she also, em, engaged staff in the factory, mainly girls, she took on. And when, if there was any problems or that with the girls or they were sick or anything like that, she used to go and visit them.

But she also visited a lot of the pensioners, I mean we still paid pensioners. They used to go up every Friday and she, she had I would say some faults, maybe many faults. But it depended on Miss Park whether an ex-employee got a pension or not. In the early days. This was, they didn't contribute to it. And it just lay in her hands and, in many ways, she made her own rules. She had a free hand in it. But if you smoked and drank, whether you were male or female, and you were relatively poor because of it, she felt sorry for you and she would recommend a pension. But if you happened to be a steady, upright citizen, and didn't do anything in excess, she said, 'Oh no, they're quite well off, so they don't need a pension.' It wasn't on the grounds of whether you'd been a good worker or a bad worker, it depended on how she thought the necessity arose to support you.

And it was only ten shillings, some got a pound, some got thirty shillings, but that was a lot really because at the outbreak of war, a printer was getting three pounds seventeen and six a week. And with his national insurance off, he finished up with three fifteen eleven. So, in relation to thinking that that was a tradesman, if somebody got a pound or thirty shillings as a pensioner, that wasn't bad going, and of course there was a period before the war where things were so bad —

I think everyone got on reasonably well with everyone else.

5

There was clear definitions of departments, you know, that there's very little chance of being any jealousy about one person getting something you didn't. Really the only bit o' jealousy, it was silly really. Miss Park, going back to Miss Park, she had a little office where she interviewed prospective employees, and it was no bigger than about this size, maybe squarer than this, and then there was an inner sanctum. And certain people, your boss was one, Sandy Herd was another, they were invited in for coffee in the morning or tea in the morning in this inner sanctum. But there was only about four or five.

And the bit was — it faced onto the, there's an open square outside, a concrete square, 'cause there was departments that side and the joiners and that, they were down there, and that led out to Parkside Terrace out that way. But above where the joiners and the engineers were, there was an outside staircase up to the loos, where the workers, that was their place, you see. Well, we had our own, I mean, on top o' that. And Sandy Herd, who was the head of the, sort o' one o' the departments further up, who had — I don't know what had happened to him, I mean he was only about five foot four but he had a stiff leg, or whether it was an artificial leg, I don't know. But, he was one o' the ones invited in and he came up one day and he says, 'You know, I've been sitting there looking out at these men going out to the loo.' He says, 'Some of them have been there over half an hour.' And he says, 'You know, somebody should do something about it.' Now there he was, sitting there himself, having his coffee and his natter now, for half an hour, but he was criticising this lad up here, he'd been up for half an hour! So that was Miss Park.

Now, after I left the counting room, I was appointed to be in charge of sheet stock and bound stock. And you obviously know what this is, because one is the printed sheet and the other is the bound copy. That was after the war. That's right, that was after the war, because when I got involved I was due six weeks' leave, I think it was, and Archie Cowan said to me, ah, 'Do you want to come back sooner?' And I said, 'Well, fair enough, I'm not doing much.' And so I came back sooner and, I'd no sooner sort of got back into my stride in the counting room, than Alec Pryce, who had been in charge of the sheet stock and the bound stock, he retired. And I got that job.

Now the sheet stock occupied a part of what was the folding and the binding department. And when there was printing orders or binding orders required off the sheets, I had to pass the necessary information to bind up the sheets, so many thousand or whatever. The reprints also was passed through the buying department, Johnny Morrison, because he in turn was involved insofar as getting more paper in, correct paper, binding material whatever.

And on occasion, because it was reprints in the main in these days, with Classics,[3] which were always prescribed for schools, some of them anyway, Dickens and people like that, when trade was slack we used to have a meeting and decide that we'd do a certain print of some of the Classics, not just for stock as such but as a reserve just to keep the machines turning. We were allowed to print fifty thousand of the Holy Bible every year. That was an agreement with the Oxford University Press. And nobody ever came to check up if we ever did reach that figure or if we doubled it or anything, you know, it was one of these peculiar things that, it just went on, whenever things were quiet we printed the Bible, but nobody ever sort of took time off to say, 'Uh uh, that's the maximum, you've got a, go easy on it.'

And then, after that, I went to London. In '57. It was a challenge. It was a promotion and it was a challenge, and I thought well, where I was in the bound stock, where do I go from there, sort of thing. On the admin side there wasn't a lot above me, because I wasn't editorial and I wasn't on the print side at all directly. So I couldn't see any great strides in that direction, so I suppose at the time I thought, well, we'll have a go. So we went down to London, and we had a year in London in furnished accommodation, which the company paid for, which was very good, and we then bought a house in Kent and we were in Kent for seven years.

The reason I went to London actually was that they'd never had anybody from head office before, and I think it got quite sloppy because it was more or less local and everybody knew everyone else, you know. And I think a lot of things needed sort of a new face on the scene, just to try and get things organised. You see this was one of their troubles. They were totally unaware. I mean Nelsons in Edinburgh could have been on the other side of the world as far as they were concerned, because they never saw anyone from Edinburgh. And all they knew was books came from Edinburgh on the shelves, but they, they never met anyone. They had a different existence altogether.

Basically, Nelsons were a reprint house. I mean that most of their income came from the Classics which went back to the year dot practically. And they also printed the Classics for our French house. I remember we had quite a big place in Paris and Tim Morgan, who during the war was a prisoner of war because he was over there, we went over to see him — Yes, we were there after the war. Tim was a Welshman originally, but he was married to a French girl and it was looked upon I think that the books were against the Nazis' thoughts and they closed the place down and he went into a prison of war. But he was fortunate. They put him in charge of the library in one of the camps, you know, because he knew all about books! So he didn't have a rough time. But, in fact, Tim Morgan's daughter did a lot of illustrations for books in our Paris house, but he used to come over periodically to see me in London and we would have a meal and that.

John Gunn

Apart from the Classics, which was the great thing, we used to do the Bible, the Holy Bible. We even did the Book o' Prayer for the Mormons at one stage. And we also did 'Royal Readers' for West Indies, big quantities. Then after the war, because West Africa was starting to develop, we engaged two editors, one was Peter Belbin, who was English. He came and he introduced a lot of new educational books. We had a little educational department upstairs off, just below the clock as was, facing down Preston Street, and he had a little staff there, educational staff. And Leslie Murby who had worked in Africa, he joined us and oh, we set up a West African subsidiary there, it was in Ghana and Nigeria, and Jim Horsburgh, he was our representative.[4] So we did very well in Africa for a period. I wouldn't like to put a figure on it. Thousands! Thousands! But it was seasonal of course, by the academic year which determined that. And of course South Africa too, before they got their independence, they became a republic anyway, we sold a lot of books to South Africa.

These used to go from Leith in containers by sea. They were packed at Parkside, in the new factory. This was built as a bindery for in the main hard-bound books, and underneath it was the stockroom and the packing department, and outside the containers arrived by lorry and were packed there and then picked up again and taken to the docks.

When I went to London in 1958 as a warehouse manager, our warehouse there was just outside London Bridge station, main station, and faced the railway arches where all the trains actually passed overhead. And even the books that went to London went by sea from Leith to London Bridge and were then transported by lorry to the warehouse and stocked there. I think it was about three days, you know, from the time of uplifting them going with the tide and the same thing at the other end.

We had a man, Dan Reid, who was warehouse manager.

This is before the war, you see. And Dan, he lived just up in Blackford Avenue, and the war came along, and when people started to go to the services, he managed to escape that. One of the reasons, I believe, maybe he did have some defect, I don't know. He wasn't terribly old, although he was older than I was at the time. Ah, he could always get whisky for Doctor Morrison, who was then Chairman. This Doctor Morrison lived at Shaw Park down in Selkirk, and I don't know where he came from, he was a very influential person however, or whether he was called on to say that it was necessary for Dan to be there — because we did produce all sorts of war things such as these streamers to confuse the enemy, dropping from the aircraft, things like that.

Ah, anyway, he managed to stay the course in Parkside for the end of the war, and then, because we were re-opening again and we would be needing representatives here, there and everywhere, the representative in Australia was playing out time, he would have retired but he kept going during the war. So Dan, he wanted to be a representative, and thought he would land this Scottish job. And they said, 'Oh well, we'll bear it in mind when the time comes.' Well, this old chap in Australia collapsed and died in Flinders Street in Melbourne, and there was a big hoo-ha went on, who could we send to replace him? And somebody talks up, 'What about Dan Reid?' So Dan, Dan Reid, he got the job with Australia when he had hoped to get the one in Scotland one way or the other! So he went there but the other strange thing about it was when he came back from his first leave, from Australia, he'd gone out via the East, and when he came back, he came back via America and he had gone round the world and yet when he stepped ashore at Heathrow, that was the first time he'd been in England! I mean, it's incredible but true!

Most of the reps were in England and Wales. I mean, we only had one Scottish representative. He covered Scotland, because obviously geographically and number-wise, you didn't require more because when you think, Menzies' was in Edinburgh,[5] and they probably ordered for all their branches, so it cut down the number of visits a rep had to go on, whereas we had reps all over the counties in England. We had one for London, we had one for greater London, and Kent, Sussex. We had Abernethy who was an Edinburgh man. He was Hampshire, and then there were, yes I'd say about eight altogether. And they in turn, they sent in their orders to the London house, and then they were transferred up to Edinburgh. And their orders were actually executed from the warehouse in London.

They were all men 'cause basically there was a fair amount of driving and by and large at that time, girls didn't, or young ladies didn't drive great distances. And of course, they had a fair amount of stock to carry about, you know, in their cases and that, which were quite weighty. So eh, being a bit old-fashioned, the firm too probably thought, well, it wasn't a lady's job to be carrying — all the things. Even the dummy copies just to show the sort of wrapper or perhaps a rough copy of the book, and a slight résumé of what the contents would be.

There was quite a lot of material shortages and we, our machines, by and large, had been going since the year dot. And because of spares not being available during the wars, they had by and large reached an age where they couldn't be repaired any more. And yet they couldn't replace them from Britain and we started getting in German machines, which sounded rather odd, particularly in the litho department.

Of course litho was pretty well in its infancy then. And the Germans seemed to have the machines and the litho department was largely rebuilt with new machinery then. And that's why eventually, because we had decent machines, we went in more for coffee table books, like cookery and Robert Carrier cookbooks and things like that.

Thomas Nelson and Sons

I don't think they tried that hard in the earlier days. They seemed to be quite happy, A, making a profit and B, just churning out the reprints. You know, I think it was only when the opposition started getting stronger and stronger, or they had to get in fresh faces and fresh ideas and try and move with the times. They had the chance of going for more getting away from the reprint name they had, because they had fresh blood in the editorial department. When I went there, we had a room, in the South Hall which was at the end next to what is now Holyrood Road or something, it used to be Park, Park Road — Yes, and there was a Dr Gunn there, no relation of mine, but there was a Doctor Gunn, Miss Yule, and Miss Shaw. Miss Shaw, she was largely in charge of children's books, but it was all sort of cut and paste she used to go in for, and of course they had these hardback, hard board books for children, for young, very young children, and we produced thousands and thousands of these, and they sold like mad everywhere. So that is when I was in the sheet and bound stock.

We also had a chap in Edinburgh, Willie Leckie. Now, I never really understood what Willie Leckie did. In the main entrance, the first door was where Ian Nelson had a little office and subsequently Ronnie Nelson[6] had, and then next door to him, with an inter-communicating door was Willie Leckie. And we also used to have a cup o' tea there, the male members of the staff. And this Willie Leckie, he was the one who attended funerals. That seemed to be his main job! He had a black jacket and trousers and he was a very nice man. In fact one of his jobs — which seems odd nowadays, usually you think in terms more of a secretary or a junior doing it – was sorting the incoming mail. I mean, there was a fair amount of incoming mail, you know, but he sort o' sorted it out for the directors and the buyers and the accounts and, you know, all this. But, apart from that, he was always immaculately groomed and when you saw him in a black coat and trousers, you knew he was going to a funeral.

There was Edinburgh Amateurs League and there were the various cups we played for. We won the championship and we won the various cups. Nelsons had racing colours once upon a time and they were what? Yellow and purple, or something awful like that, and they used to have jerseys similar to that and I thought they were horrible so I says, 'Oh well, we'll get a brochure and see what colours we could get'. So, the fact that eventually decided me, my name was Gunn and the Arsenal team were known as the Gunners, so I says, 'Right. They'll have red shirts with white sleeves.' So I wrote off to the firm in England and got a set o' jerseys and they came up. And white pants. Up to that time, when the game was over, all the players just got their kit and stuffed it in their bags with their dirty boots and all the rest, and took them home. Well, the majority of them had them washed for the following Saturday, but some of them if they thought they weren't too dirty, turned up in dirty kits, and I didn't like that. So, in a moment o' weakness, I asked Alexia [his wife], 'What about washing the shirts, the kit for the boys?' So, eventually, she agreed to do it. Well, there was eleven shirts, eleven pair o' pants. They had to wash their own stockings. The first time we washed these jerseys the white sleeves turned out the same colour, or halfway to the red. So I wrote back and I objected strongly to the fact that the washing instructions didn't make it clear, you know, so we got a new strip back. They always had a team there.

And they had a groundsman there, George Hill. I think he was, I don't know if he was retired or what but he wasn't a young man. But if it rained on Friday, he would be into my office to say, 'I think it'll be unplayable tomorrow,' you know. 'I won't be able to mark out the pitch,' you know. Any excuse at all, put the game off. It was too wet for him to walk out and mark the lines. But no, it was successful, probably after I left to go to London, I don't know, but we all had a good time. We used to also arrange for bus trips through to the cup ties, Hearts were playing and things like that, in Glasgow, you know. Anybody, the employees, because I remember Hearts beat Celtic in the final one year — and, what was his name from Prestonfield. He was standing at the outside o' the bus, when we got back to Edinburgh, standing on the step o' the bus and he was throwing his money out, so delighted that Hearts had won the cup! And I thought, 'You'll regret it tomorrow when you sober up!'

Everybody had a dance, you know, the tennis club, the bowling club, the football club, so in the winter, it was always a Friday night. And you used to have a succession of functions like that almost every week.

Annual trips. Often we used to go — I arranged them as well. Well, we'd a committee, but we used to go to Rothesay and we went to, well, we went down to England — aye, aye, winter sail down to Rothesay on one occasion. But it was a more wider thing because it was the works as well, just the same as the annual dance which was in the Assembly Rooms. There's a committee of representatives from the office and the works who made decisions like that.

What we used to do was, we had a rep from the railway come up, you see? And they used to do a special price for us obviously and you'd sort o' narrow it down to say Rothesay, Wemyss Bay, it could be some place in the North of England — Whitley Bay, we went to Whitley Bay one year. And sort of amongst the committee, get an opinion and then the railway chappie, he would come up and he'd say, 'Well, I can do a hundred and fifty for so much, two hundred for so on.' And we also left it to them to suggest places that we could eat while we were there. I mean, if we were going the cruise down to Rothesay, he would say, 'Well, we can fix you up on the boat for a lunch and mibby a high tea in this hotel.' And give us an overall price for the day's outing per head.

And we then sort of put it to the committee to ask amongst the people who would be interested in going here, there or everywhere, and then, when a decision was made, we just said, 'This has been arranged and anyone interested, pay their representative the money.' But it was subsidised, it was subsidised — it wasn't much — oh no, because we always got a tremendous number of people going, you know. But it was always a successful do.

We used to have a library in the staff up there, and you all paid, oh I forget, some ridiculous low sum, maybe half a crown or something a month. I would say twenty mibby, twenty-five in the book club, and everybody got a turn and when it was your turn you were allowed to buy books to the value of x pounds and whatever titles you wanted. And it was understood that you could only have one to read right away, put the rest in the book club and other people got the same chance o' reading. And then eventually, when it was felt that they were old — or when everybody had read it, you got the book back. But this was only amongst the staff. But whether that still carried on after we left, I don't know.

For a long time the print unions, they were a very hostile thorn in the eyes of the management. You know they used to make agreements for three years. The management always pushed for a longer agreement. For obvious reasons, they thought they'd get peace for three years or more and accordingly tried to judge what pay they were gonna pay them. And of course the unions, it's rather like footballers today. They wanted a shorter agreement so that they could come that much sooner to raise the ante, you see. Although it probably cut both ways because with uncertainty in the amount of work going on, you could cut your own throat, because they might have to lay off people, whereas if they're on for three years, they're safer that way than a shorter period.

But there was always the threat of a stoppage in the pipeline or if there was any justification for someone being sacked or suspended or that. It was all right when they were busy. There was never any sort of threat of stoppages if there's plenty overtime going but when things got quieter, there was always looking for an excuse to have a battle. It was generally the trade rather than the actual Nelsons. Nelsons weren't too bad that way. You see, one of the things too, they were quite selective because they were only allowed to engage so many apprentices according to the total of journeymen, that you almost had to wait for someone to leave, die or retire or whatever before you could get somebody else in. And again, it was usually somebody in the family or somebody's relative who was pushed forward to start their time. But once in Nelsons, they rarely left to go to another printer.

I think the turning point really came when Thomsons took over.[7] His idea, apparently, if one was to believe the story of the time, was that he felt he should have a Scottish publisher and I think he had his eyes on Nelsons. But I think it was a case from Nelsons point of view, if we didn't join him, he could have gone to Blackies[8] or to someone else, and taken them over which would have been detrimental to Nelsons, whereas anyone in the educational field, they could throw his weight behind them financially and Nelsons would have lost out, so I think, from Nelsons point of view —

Well it was the funniest thing really. I got a phone call from Ian Carriline. He was the accountant who succeeded Mr Harding, and he phoned me and he said, 'There's to be a meeting. Ah, you no doubt have seen it in the newspapers this morning that we may be taken over. Can you come up?' So I flew up and there was a meeting addressed by Dr Morrison, in the canteen. And he spoke out, Leslie Murby by this time was a director, Bob Cairns was a director. And they were all on the top table, and Dr Morrison sort of told them all how wonderful it was going to be, and how Lord Thomson would do this for the firm and that for the firm, and nobody would be made redundant and the board would carry on as normal. And within a short space of time, Bob Cairns had gone, Leslie Murby went to Collins, and that was the break-up of the board.

I don't know who succeeded them after that, and then I had a phone call, say — Oh, we went up to Leslie — Leslie Murby lived in Ramsay Gardens, up at the castle, he had a marvellous flat up there and we were at a party there with Lord Thomson and Brunton, who was his right-hand man then, and one or two others from Thomsons, and there they were, all glad-handing us and, you know, everything was going to be fine and it wouldn't be all that bad and all the rest. And I went back to London then, and I had a phone call one day saying, um, this chap Jocelyn Baines would like to come over and see me, he was an editor who was joining Nelsons from Thomsons. And we had lunch together. When we met he met me as an editor, and the next time I saw him he was my managing director! You know, just like that, out o' the blue! And it's rather difficult because if you are speaking to someone just about business in a general way, sort of on equal terms, you may say a lot of things which you might regret. If you were introduced to him as your new managing director, you might think, well, I'll better bite on that for a wee while to see which way he's gonna swing. But Jocelyn was a gem of a person.

Also, Ian Nelson had died in the meantime, and Ronnie Nelson was the only Nelson left there. He was never happier than when he was on the footplate of a train. He had permission and you know nowadays when you think back to this recent rail disaster, you felt how on earth could he be allowed to be on a footplate of a train, an express going from Edinburgh to London. I mean, he wasn't in the rail union, he had no authority to be there but he used to have three stop-watches and he used to time it from here to Dalkeith, and

Dalkeith to Newcastle, and send in a report to the LMS, LNER, whoever. And then when he got to London, if he wasn't happy with his stop-watches, he used to say to, to me, 'Would you take a taxi up, there's a specialist firm up at Tottenham Court Road.' And he says, 'Pop them in and ask them to check on their accuracy,' you know. And he said, 'I'll be here until Friday so tell them I must have it back by Friday.'

Sometimes you got a phone call from Edinburgh saying he was coming, other times he arrived and because of trains in London, you might be a few minutes late, and the first thing he did, he would go in and say, 'Oh good morning, Sir, indeed', as if to say, 'I've caught you out again', you know! You couldn't start saying, well, the train was held up, because, you know, it sounded a lame excuse. He was a great Conservative too, you know, he used to go to all the Conservative conferences and all the rest.

So we were taken over by Lord Thomson. I feel he was just an asset-stripper basically. I mean he wasn't as bad as Robert Maxwell, but he bought Nelsons. And then where the Commonwealth Pool is, of course, that was our sports ground, where the girls played hockey on occasion. There was a pitch and putt golf course, there was football, there was tennis courts, and of course the bowling club which still exists. But the first thing he did practically was sell that off to the Council. Ah, I don't know what he got for it, or why he did it even. And then of course he proceeded to close down the factory, the works in fact. Quite a number I think got work in Thynes, they went to Thynes to work.[9] And of course they sold that too because it was Scottish Widows, so he really made a pile one way and another.

But then, I don't know what started to go wrong. But a few people came down from Edinburgh, but mainly on the office side. There was Allan Ramsay and his wife. They were young. I mean, he only did national service, you know, after the war, so he was that much younger. Peter Belbin came down, who was the educational editor, but he was English anyway.

So Peter Belbin came down, Ian Carriline came down to be the chief accountant. And he moved into Park Street with me, and Jocelyn Baines, by this time he had been appointed Managing Director. So basically, the head office was in Park Street, and then Ian Carriline one day was introduced to someone who was going to be the chief accountant, you know, that sort of approach! And they had a publicity manager, Jonathan Curling, who was also a director. And they had managers who did the publicity of advertising in other newspapers and that sort of thing, and the cashier who was there who attended to the wages for the warehouse. And I was there and had to greet people and arrange conferences for the various things, like when the representatives had their annual meetings and got told all the forthcoming books and things like that and attend conferences.

We had to find a new warehouse, just after the takeover and it was obvious that they were gonna move from Edinburgh and they were sounding out people who were gonna be prepared to move to the south. And some of the people obviously didn't want to go because of their age. And with commitments in Edinburgh. Others again, young, there was talk that they'd found them housing —

So it fell to me to start hunting for warehousing and they didn't want it in London particularly. They wanted it further out, if necessary near motorways. They were thinking obviously on transport to ports or inland, and I looked various places. I looked at one in Harlow in Essex, which was a new town starting up then. And they were offering, their council were offering housing, sort a' two grades of housing, one for workers and one for admin staff and that if we took up the offer, which we didn't. I mean, we discussed it, what advantage going that way to Essex, it was sort of further away from Liverpool or the north or wherever.

And finally, we found one, down in Sunbury-on-Thames, which was a new development going up, a new industrial estate.[10] And it seemed ideal for the M4 motorway, it was ideal for Heathrow for freight, and again it was convenient for London. So because of that, we moved from Kent over to just outside Staines and we were there for twenty years. And so we set up the warehouse there.

George Sweeney, when I left the sheet stock and bound stock in Edinburgh, he had been my assistant. And he took over the job in charge of the warehouse at Sunbury, the setting up of the stocks there, because there was a much bigger stock. Previously, at Parkside, it had been divided, simply because of the space, in various parts of the building according to how big the stocks were, if it was getting near Christmas or the academic year, things like that. So, it tended to be pushed into any place they could take it, whereas this was a completely new stockholding warehouse. So he did that job, and did it exceptionally well, I think.

I could feel things changing as well, from my point of view, you know. It wasn't a happy atmosphere to be in. It was all — it was a bit of an undercurrent, you know. And anyway, I answered an advertisement for a Finance Officer at the Girls' Public Day School Trust. But, if you think in terms of what is now, it was girls' schools, private girls' schools. And at that time, we had twenty-six schools in England and, oh, we certainly took over one in Wales too. I left Nelsons then and worked there for seventeen years in Queen Anne's Gate, which is just really adjacent to the House of Commons, in London. So I continued to work in London for another seventeen years.

So it was very sad, such a turnover of people that you knew in a short space of time. You can't look back, or you shouldn't look back. You should look forward, but the strange thing is when Nelsons was on the go, I suppose this was common to almost everybody who worked in Nelsons, you couldn't walk from here to Surgeons Hall[11] without meeting probably a dozen people who worked in Nelsons, if it was just to say 'Hello' in the passing. You know, now, because we're all old, there may be half that number, still walking back and forward in that area, and yet I wouldn't know them and they wouldn't know me.

Notes

1 Heriot-Watt College, Chambers Street, Edinburgh, became Heriot-Watt University.
2 For a history of the Nelson family and their work in the firm, see Introduction above. For further reading: Ramsay, Allan. *Nelson the Publisher*, Walton-on-Thames: Thomas Nelson and Sons, 1981; *'Nelsons' of Edinburgh. A Short History of the Firm, Reprinted from 'The British Printer'*, nd (c1911); Slaven, Anthony and Checkland, Sydney, eds, *Dictionary of Scottish Business Biography 1860–1960. Volume 2. Processing, Distribution, Services*, Aberdeen: Aberdeen University Press, 1990, 200–202; McCleery, Alistair. 'Thomas Nelson and Sons'. In Anderson, Patricia J and Rose, Jonathan, eds, *British Literary Publishing Houses, 1820–1880. Dictionary of Literary Biography. Volume 106*. Detroit: Gale Research, 1990, 218–224; Dempster, John A H. 'Thomas Nelson & Sons in the late nineteenth century: a study in motivation', *Publishing History*, 13 (1983), 41–87; 14 (1983), 5–63.
3 Classics, a series of reprints of 'classic' fiction by writers such as Thackeray, Dickens and Buchan.
4 In Africa, Nelsons opened a branch in Lagos in 1961 and one in Nairobi in 1963. See introduction, xx.
5 John Menzies, publishers and wholesalers of books, periodicals and newspapers. The firm was recognised as a Scottish institution, selling its products at railway book stalls and in high street stores.
6 Ronnie Nelson was the son of Ian Nelson. See introduction, xx.
7 Lord Thomson of Fleet.
8 Blackie & Sons, founded in Glasgow.

Thomas Nelson and Sons

9 William Thyne of Edinburgh, carton maker and manufacturing stationer.
10 The publishing side of Nelsons moved to Walton on Thames, Surrey, in late 1962. Nelsons in Edinburgh traded as Thomas Nelson (Printers) Limited. See introduction, xx.
11 Surgeons' Hall, home of the Royal College of Surgeons, Nicholson Street, Edinburgh.

BOB SINCLAIR

I can't remember the date I first started work. It would be 1954, in the August, I'm sure, having left school at the age of fifteen in probably the last week of June, first week of July when schools closed. I went round, I think I went to the union, I think that's where I went. And I got a list of all the companies that were affiliated to the union. Oh, there might have been about thirty or forty companies in Edinburgh at that time. And I went round asking, 'Have you any apprenticeships coming along? I'd like to get a job in the print trade.' Well at that time, Edinburgh was known for the three B's: beer, books and biscuits. And so there were a lot of people employed in printing, although I don't know if I ever knew anyone else in the print trade. But it was talk, shall we say, 'What are you going to work at?' Anyone leaving school at fifteen was going into a trade, they weren't going on to further education. And the print trade was generally regarded as a fairly good industry to be in. And I think it was regarded as paying fairly good wages. So, for whatever reason, I went round all the different print companies asking if there were any vacancies and the answer was 'No, no, no, no, no.' And then I remember one lad in a wee print shop: 'Oh, I can't afford the time and the money to send laddies off to college for day release classes.' So that was a negative attitude and I thought, 'Well, I'm glad that you've not got a vacancy. I don't want a job here.'

And eventually, up at Nelsons, they said, 'Yes, we've got a vacancy.' I have a faint recollection of the man who interviewed me who was very much a gentlemanly, quiet-spoken man. I've forgotten his name, a white-haired man, and he said to me, 'We have two vacancies. One in the Caseroom' — No, beg your pardon, that's not what he said. He said, 'We have one vacancy as a compositor and another as a letterpress printer.' And I said, 'Well, I would be interested in the compositor's position.' And I think maybe what had made me think along those lines was as a youngster at school, which was Moray House School in Edinburgh, I'd been taken on a school visit to Oliver and Boyds who weren't too far from there, up in St Mary's Street, and having gone round the printworks and seen the various departments, they had asked our names when we first went in and by the time we left they'd set our names up in type and we were given a proof of it before we left. And the floor, in between the cracks of the floorboards, all these bits o' metal type were lying, and I think it perhaps just caught my imagination. However, when I eventually had gone to Nelsons and they said they had this vacancy for an apprentice compositor, I said that's what I would be interested in. And at the same time as I was making this approach, there was another chap and it so happened that he was interested in being a letterpress printer.

In those days, they sent you up to Edinburgh University[1] and they gave you a wee IQ type o' test putting round pegs into square holes and so on. And colour blindness tests, that type of thing. And word came back to go and visit Nelsons again, and when I went there, I was told I'd passed the examination and that they would like to offer me this apprenticeship with them. But when I spoke with the man, he said, 'We're pleased to offer you the apprenticeship in the Caseroom.' And this was a term I hadn't heard before and I think my jaw must have dropped because I could see by the look on his face that he hadn't quite anticipated that reaction. When he said 'Caseroom', I imagined someone making wooden crates for despatch, export, things going overseas and so on. Just the word case had put that into my mind, little realising that a case was where the type was held, stored. So when he said that to me, I said, 'I thought you were offering me a vacancy as an apprentice compositor.' And he said, 'Yes, I am.' He said, 'A compositor works in the Caseroom,' and that clarified the situation.

But the apprenticeship wasn't to start immediately, it wasn't to start until the eleventh of November, so it was an easy date to remember throughout my lifetime. I started my apprenticeship on the eleventh of November, which was Remembrance Day. But they did offer me a job as a wee sort of message boy going round the offices and collecting and uplifting and depositing mail in the various trays and so on. Which was quite good, because it gave me an idea now of what the layout of the place was and I met the different people in various departments between the offices and in the works. So that I appreciated. I worked at that for, I don't know, from say sometime in August up until the November when I started my apprenticeship.

The one disappointing thing initially was he'd said to me, 'It's a well-paid job, this position in the front office.' I told him, I think I had imagined at that time it might have been worth about three pounds or three pounds fifty a week and to my disappointment it was only about half that. However, I accepted it. I thought it'd keep me interested and give me an insight into what the place was like in total, and then I started my apprenticeship in November.

When I started I think the working week had dropped to forty-four and a half hours. A year before I think it had been forty-six or forty-seven, and I think the year prior to that, they had you working on a Saturday morning, a five and a half day week. So I walked into a five day week and two weeks holidays in the year, and those were fixed holidays at Edinburgh Trades, the first two weeks of July. I think most folk kind o' complained that they were forced to take their holidays at that time of the year, and they didn't have variable holidays when they can take them when they wanted. It was all just the thought of well, if it rains during those two weeks, wherever I go, I've had it. Rather get a choice perhaps.

They had their usual initiation for new apprentices coming into the place. I recall being chased around the place and getting caught and one section, as you made your approach into the Caseroom from the yard, where the lorries used to bring in paper and ink and whatever else, as you made your way from a corridor into the Caseroom, you had to go up three or four steps. There was a space under the Caseroom floor at that point of maybe something like four feet, shall we say. And at the bottom of the stairs, there was a wee hatch door thing, and I remember getting caught and pushed in through this door under the floors. And it was all stoury under there and the folk were walkin' on the floor above you, the stour kept on dropping down the cracks between the floorboards and if you looked up you were getting dust in your eyes, and you were coughing and spluttering and such. And I remember lying on my back and kicking like hell with my toes on the floorboards, whereas that just forced more dust through on top of me. Obviously I was making such a racket. The Caseroom had a thoroughfare for anyone from the offices going into other parts of the factory and quite regularly the Works Managers and others, Directors and such, would be passing through, so obviously they wouldnae want them to hear this noise going on, so I think I wasn't under the floorboards very long. I think I was allowed out quite quickly.

Oh it happened to others, aye! I can't remember any others going under the floorboards when I was there, but I think I'd heard that others had been under the floor as I had been. And then, the stone — it was a table. I would describe it best as being a table which had maybe about an inch thick of steel on the top and that's where all the type was worked on, and the pages were imposed in their correct sequence with the correct margins between each page. There was a metal frame around it and it was locked up with what we called quoins, and the spaces between the pages was called furniture. It was all locked up so it could be lifted up as one piece, maybe anything from four pages up to thirty-two pages within this metal frame. And it was obviously a very heavy thing — four square inches of type, ie a line or lines of type four inches wide by an inch deep, weighed a pound in weight, so sixteen or thirty-two pages of type in a forme was a fair hefty weight, maybe over a hundredweight or something. So we used to have to lift these up and down onto this metal top table thing called a stone. However, when they would clear a stone, nothing on it at all, some poor unfortunate apprentice would be grabbed, lifted onto the stone, placed on their back and ropes would be tied round their hands and their feet, hands pulled above their head backwards. Underneath this table top there were drawers which ran the full way from one side to the other, and the ropes were tied round the handles on each side o' this thing so when they pulled their legs their hands went back, and when they pulled their hands their legs went back. They couldnae move and that was them stuck on top of this stone and you can probably well imagine what sort of things happened to them!

Still there was also another use, socially, in this respect. We used to have games of shove ha'penny on it. They were very smooth, very slidy. It was like a kind of football game with a wee bar o' metal at either end and two people would have a penny each and the ha'penny would be the ball and you used to flick the penny with your finger onto the ha'penny and try and score, try and strike this wee metal bar at the far end to score a goal. We used to do this during our lunch break.

The stones that we had varied in size. Our stones were probably about five foot long, maybe six foot long at the most by say five feet deep. And they came up to maybe stomach height which would be, what? Three and a half feet. In the winter-time they were very cold, 'cause you had to lean against them when you were working and of course the cold used to catch you in the stomach. In summertime, they were nice and cool. Short-sleeved shirts on and such you could lean on them and the steel would keep you cool.

The apprenticeship had just been reduced to six years and within the previous two or three years I think it had been seven. During that apprenticeship period we attended night-school for three nights a week during winter months and a day release class one day per week up at the Heriot-Watt in Chambers Street, opposite the national museum. I think that lasted for three years and that was compulsory and thereafter it was purely voluntary. I continued evening classes until I was about twenty-seven which took me up to the Full Technological certificate standard in printing. By that time I'd actually left Nelsons. There was another lad, he was a letterpress printer and Peter Masterton was his name, and at that time I think he and I were possibly the only two that I can remember that had carried on as far into nightschool classes, for as long a period shall we say, after our apprenticeship or the compulsory attendance at nightschool ended.

The Works Manager at the time, a chap Bobby Hogg, was one of our teachers at the college, and I remember both Peter and I had made an approach to him saying, you know, what opportunities are likely to arise in the office within Nelsons in Edinburgh, that would maybe give us a job off the factory floor. And at that time he said, 'Well, there's nothing in the offing.' He says, 'You just never know what's round the corner, of course'. 'But,' he says, 'at this moment,' he says, 'there's nothing I can truthfully make an offer that might be of interest to you.' And he says, 'Of course I do realise that in those circumstances, there's a good chance that you could just leave and find an opportunity elsewhere.' Which did happen. Peter went over to Canada, and I left and moved to another company in Edinburgh. At the time I was the youngest apprentice a chap called Jack Osborne was the senior apprentice. Jack had moved on from Nelsons at one point, and it was he, in actual fact who came back to me to say, 'Look, are you interested in a move off the factory floor? There's a position I know that's gonna come up and I could maybe speak for you.' So that was how it all started for me to, shall we say, begin a career as such in printing and publishing.

At the end of the day, I had to prove, I suppose, that it was worthwhile going to classes, that it was going to show some value at the end of the day. At the day release class I won some prize, a Scottish Typographical Association prize, and I think I could buy something to a certain value and I bought two or three books, a dictionary and some other books relative to the printing trade. And then I did an estimating course. I thought, if I'm going to move off the factory floor, I've got to get away from the production side into adminis-tration tasks, so I did an estimating course. Possibly that helped me to get into the job as an estimator later on. And then, taking further classes to Full Technological standard, to a degree maybe opened the door for interviews for other jobs. Once you get the interview, it's up to you what you do at that stage, you know.

Yes, I would say it was worth spending the time in doing what I did. I never had any regrets there. In the first year of evening classes, as I say, we did three nights. One night was a keep-fit class. Another night was for English, and our third night was theory and practical comp work. I don't know whether it was fit in body, fit in mind or something. It was three years we did nightschool and in the first year only we did that keep-fit class. And I think the second and the third year, it dropped to two nights.

There was term exams, or term tests anyway, you know, exams, term tests, and then an exam at the end of the session and you were given a certificate which also showed attendance. Those that were poor attenders, if you maybe skipped three nights or something, they would send off a note to the company, 'cause I can remember some lads bein' reprimanded from the foreman, not in Nelsons but in other companies — being reprimanded for missing nightschool classes. There might have been a football match on or something, or they just decided not to come along.

I remember the day-release class at the Heriot-Watt. It was quite a small class, so, maybe about twelve if I remember rightly, in whatever year it was. And we had an English session there. A chap Reid was the teacher. He went to Newbattle College[2], I remember him telling us. I found those classes quite stimulating, and I think I was a wee bit fortunate. I got in with a crowd o' chaps who were quite bright. As a consequence, it possibly pulled me along with it, you know. I would think the majority of those lads, for sure, all moved away from comping into administration jobs.

They were a keen bunch o' lads, keen to learn, willing to put an effort into it. The chap Reid, the English teacher, commented on one occasion that he thought it was probably the best class he'd ever had in being attentive and applying themselves to the work that we were given to do. On one occasion, he said to us, 'I think your standard is so high, at this stage, I'm not going to give you a term test. I'm happy that the standard you're doing is far in excess of what I'd have to test you on to try and find out what level you are attaining.' I remember doing some work for the class, I cannae think of what it was. A friend of mine was at university and he was assisting me in doing something or other, and I think he was quite surprised at what I was doing as a compositor at the Heriot-Watt. And he thought, 'Oh, I'm surprised that you're doing something to a standard of that level for someone who is not at university.' So what was taught there was quite a high standard and certainly in particular our class had responded to him.

The lads that I attended college with, they were all, shall we say ambitious? Ambitious to move from what they were doing and try and make some progress up the ladder into management, therefore they were all looking for moves, and maybe they had made a first move and if a better one came along, again, we were quite prepared to move again. Within the composing field I would say I saw a fair number of lads coming into Nelsons. I don't remember so very many leaving to be honest with you, but certainly I would say the size of the Caseroom staff increased whilst I was there.

The first year we were given a lot of mundane tasks to do, whereas at the same time it gave you the opportunity of going around chatting with the senior or more senior apprentices or journeymen, and basically asking questions. 'What are you doing this for?', 'Why are you doing this?', and 'What's it for?', the usual inquisitive questions you're likely to ask. That coupled with your introductory class at the night school introduced you to proper composing as such in your second year. Six years you could say was too long, and certainly now it has been reduced to modules.

At one point in my apprenticeship, say maybe about my third or fourth year, they began to print one or two small jobs directly from the type itself, and luckily for me, I was the one that was asked to do that part of it. Make up the pages and the formes and take them through to lift them onto the printing press and so forth. And that introduced a bit more interest for me rather than just making up the pages and having them sent through to the foundry for the duplicate plates to be made, which would be either stereos or electros.

At one point, I and the other apprentices were dissatisfied with the training that we were being given. Having spent the first year not doing any composing work, second and third years having an introduction to it but saying to myself, am I going to get the opportunity later in my apprenticeship to get on a keyboard, get on the casting machine, get on the linotype, get an opportunity to do some reading because I was aware that some of the older apprentices than me hadn't had that opportunity and they were maybe in their fifth and sixth year still more or less doing the same as what I was doing. So, between ourselves we all agreed that we were dissatisfied and that we had to speak out about it in the hope that something would be done — and it was. It was only a matter of communication. We didn't see there were any formalised training schedule so we spoke amongst ourselves, spoke to the foreman and eventually there was an agreed schedule set up for us to spend a period of time doing different aspects, different areas of the composition work which might be so much working on the stone, a certain amount of time on the keyboard and the monotype casting machine. And we also had a linotype machine.

When working on the stone as an apprentice you started off by doing the corrections. And then it might be merely house corrections, ie keyboard operator making some error so it was proofread. Those would be corrected and then another proof taken to be sent out back to the editor with the original copy for them to do their proof reading and whatever else — maybe editing.

It was all very time-consuming. The average line, for comfortable reading, had ten or eleven words. The average word including a space had five, six characters, and when it initially came off the casting machine, the space between each word was one single piece. When you went to do a correction, you were maybe putting the character of a different width from what you were taking out, that line could either be too long or too short, so you then had to adjust the spacing. So by taking out the space between the words, we had wee boxes with variable spaces in them. The normal measurement was an em, E-M, for mother. If you take it in twelve point, for example, it was twelve point square. Half of that was an en, E-N for nothing, and then you had a third of that, what you called a space three. You had a quarter and a fifth space of that em. And you could use multiples of those variations and start off with the third which we called a thick. To go up from that it was a four and a five and then, oh I forgot now, let me think, there was a five, a four, a thick, a four and a five and then it was up to an en, then you were up to a thick and a five, two thicks and you build it up, until you got back up to a full em.

And you would hardly want an em space between words but you could vary that, and that variation was a matter of guesswork. Experience would tell you what you thought might be the correct spacing to put between each of those words to try and justify the line to the correct width. But you had a wee bit guddle around sometimes to get the correct spaces until you got that line the same width as all the others, the one preceding it and the one after it. Because if in actual fact when it was locked up in the forme and it wasn't the exact width, if it was too long, pressure from the side on the page would bite on that long line and the lines above and below it could drop out, or if it was too short, the words and spaces within that line could drop out.

So it was essential that you had it exactly the same width as the others round about it. When you were varying the space between those words, which might be as a result of a bad break, a bad hyphenation in one of the lines, you had to adjust it to look better. Or maybe you would get what you used to call rivers of space running through a page or a paragraph and you wanted to amend that, you had to re-justify these lines. Or when you were maybe making up a page and you had what we used to call orphan lines or widow lines and you wanted to get rid of those, you had to re-justify lines. You would be looking for, say for example if a 'd' at the end of one word came against an 'l' as the first letter of the next word, you would increase the space between that word greater than you would where you had a word ending in a 'y' and the next one beginning in a 'w' because of the cutaway shape of those characters. So you would look along the line to find out what characters were coming adjacent to each other, and then you would vary your spacing accordingly. So you had to keep your eyes open on what you were doing. There was no rules as such, or maybe unwritten rules, and if you didn't follow that format and re-proofed it, at a later date it would become so obvious when you saw it on the next proof that the space between the 'y' and 'w' was so great in comparison to the 'd' and the 'l' that you would realise right away: 'Oh no, I've got to decrease the space there and increase it there.' It became second nature to do it.

There was jobs that you didn't want to do and there was jobs that you wanted to do. Particularly I think the apprentices wanted to make the galleys of type up into page form. We used to call them cleakers, that was the guys made the pages up and the type up into pages — the cleakers. And everybody wanted that job. That was a kind o' prestige job. So apprentices normally started off working under a journeyman after they'd gone through this elementary stage of correction and so forth. They were assigned to work with a journeyman.

But they got all the navvying jobs of course, bringing the galleys of type from the racks up to the frames before the pages were made up. After the journeymen had made the pages into the correct depth with whatever had to go in, in the way of an illustration and verse and whatever else, footnotes and so on, the apprentice had to lift the pages, maybe tie them up with what we called page cord, and you used to wrap this round each page and lift it onto the stone to impose it in the sequence for correct folding purposes. Then they had to collect the furniture, the correct width of furniture between each page for its head margin, its back margin, its gutters and its tails and so on. Place that in, place the chase — this was the metal frame round about it, sidestick, footstick the quoins — and then take the page cord off, tighten all this up, knock up the quoins with a mallet and what they called a shooting stick, a flat piece of wood.

You put this plane over the page, lines of type, and tap it with a mallet, generally a leather-headed mallet, so that all the characters were level, none were protruding higher than the others, and tighten this up so it could be lifted off as one piece. And this was lifted off and trundled away, put into rack just awaiting a further proof to be taken in page forme. So the apprentices were often given all these navvying jobs, but it was part o' the process of the trade and learning. Then obviously the journeyman would say, 'Come and see what I'm doing. I'm doing this' and you would be shown what he was doing, why he was doing it and then you would get the opportunity of doing that next time around and this was how you learnt.

I found the journeymen very helpful, encouraging. You know, they would say, 'Stick in at your night school class, you're doing the right thing if you want to move up in the world', or whatever, 'Aye, stick in.' Oh, I found the journeymen to my liking. Like in any other field, the human element varies and you get a few disgruntled guys and some other people are maybe just a wee bit better at teaching than others and they had a different personality. And I would say that there were some journeymen that were better than others. There was journeymen that had wee competitions between themselves. 'I'm better than you,' you know, 'I'm faster than you', sort a' thing. We used to have a wee race with the same type of work. Let's see how many pages we can make up and impose within an hour or so. Of course, the poor apprentice, he was the one that got the hard task of keepin' up with the journeyman! But aye, it was a bit o' good humour and a bit of good fun.

Thomas Nelson and Sons

In general terms, I didn't think it was a particularly interesting Caseroom to work in. Having mixed with lads from other commercial sort o' companies, mixing with them at day classes and evening classes, I always felt they had a much more interesting job as a compositor than what I had. Probably they had more opportunity to use their own, shall we say, artistic talent, maybe just designing a dance ticket or a poster or something along those lines, a leaflet or something like that. Whereas ours was basic bookwork of a headline, some text and a folio as a very basic page. I think occasions arose where you could use your own initiative and come up with a suggestion as an alternative, and I think that did arise from time to time. Probably not very often but it did arise, I'm sure.

I thought Nelsons were a wee bit antiquated in their composition area. It didn't thrill me anyway. I can recall as an apprentice there was a room, a fair, fair-sized room with a good height of ceiling that contained racks, well no, I don't suppose racks would be a term. From the floor up to perhaps the height of ten feet there were cupboards with shallow trays, maybe only just over an inch high because type height's 0.918" and these shallow drawers were just deep enough to take line illustrations — well, they wouldn't be line illustrations, they were hand-carved wood engravings. And so you can imagine something of the height of roughly about ten feet with drawers only an inch deep, from bottom to top, and they would be how long? Must have been, there were rows of maybe twelve feet long. And I don't know how many rows there were but there were certainly about ten or twelve rows of these drawers containing all those wood engravings. They wanted to clear this room which they eventually made into a small room for the composing staff which I worked in with an apprentice, a younger apprentice, and eventually with an older journeyman who came over from Canada.

There weren't many machines in the composing room. The

readers were sitting in wee tiny cubicles, with a seat and a wee desk. The desk was at an angle and wasnae particularly wide and they would sit one behind each other. I think there were about six or seven readers. And on the left-hand side was a glass partition where they could see into the main composing room. The monotype keyboard operators, and there were three or four, they were in another wee area that was sectioned off, again with a glass partition. You could see into them but that was principally because they were partitioned off because of noise. Adjacent to them was the linotype machine, which once again was partitioned off separately. The monotype casters were just outside the area of both keyboards, monotype and linotype, that was a very noisy thing. And you could hear that noise drifting back into the general Caseroom, but I mean it wasn't disturbing. Far enough away not to be too loud.

I only had training on the casting machine. In fact, I can't think of any of the lads at my time who had training on both keyboard and casting. It was one or the other, and I don't think it was a choice. I think we were just told, 'You're being trained on the caster, you're being trained on the keyboards.' I went to evening classes for two years for the caster, in addition to the six months, nine months perhaps, in-house training in Nelsons. It was a noisy machine and really quite a complex machine. I was quite interested in it in the respect of its mechanical side. It was like, it was like a watch, all those moving parts that were levers moving back and forwards just above each other and so forth.

I remember one of the Monotype engineers that used to come in from time to time. He had hands like shovels and how he actually managed to get his fingers into some of the wee spaces to reach some of the parts that he had to, I really don't know, because I've not got big hands and at times trying to get my fingers into some of these places was really quite difficult. It was a dangerous machine. We had this wee pot of molten metal, this composition — I can't remember its temperature to be honest with you. But it was in a molten state and there was a pump which used to pump this metal up through a wee nozzle into the mould for each character. And sometimes something would go wrong and what they would used to term a splash — the molten metal would come out and would splash out and there would be a jam between the matrix case and the top of this nozzle. When the metal splashed out on you, it'd maybe get on your hand or some-thing, on your arms if you didn't have any sleeves rolled down. By golly, it used to burn you! You sometimes peeled off this bit of silver metal, and there'd be a white mark on your hand. But it was short and sharp. A very intricate bit of equipment I would have said.

You used a micrometer to gauge the width of a typeface. You had Baskerville, Bodoni, Perpetua, all those different typefaces. The width of the typeface varied and you would take a letter 'M', capital 'M', and it was a certain width, and you used to use the micrometer to get this width accurate. And we used an eyeglass to set the height of the character on the body, you would use a capital 'H'. You had a master letter and you would compare the height of the master one against the new one that you were just going to start casting. You used to align the bar of the letter 'H', one against the other so that they were in the perfect position because at some later date, if you were making corrections, whether it be house corrections or editorial alterations, and you were dropping in new characters and new words, but particularly when you were just dropping in one character at a later date, then obviously the alignment of all those characters had to be spot on.

By checking the width of your letter 'M', that then set the width of all the other characters in the alphabet because the letter 'I' would be maybe five units and the other characters would be ten units, fourteen, fifteen, twenty units until you

Bob Sinclair

got up to your widest character, like a 'W', you know. So, they set the width for that specific typeface in that type size.

There were books that Monotype published that I used in later years. When I moved on from Nelsons to a job where I was calculating how many pages a manuscript would make in a certain typeface, sometimes it was a matter of, 'We want to have a book of x amount of pages', so you had to work backwards. You had to select a typeface that was going to give you so many pages. So you first of all maybe calculated it in one typeface and you were going to be pages short, but you could alter it in various ways. You could either increase your type size, maybe make it twelve point instead of eleven point. You could increase the space between the lines. You could narrow the width of the lines which would carry words forward to make more lines. You could start every new chapter on the right-hand page which would maybe mean the last page of the preceding chapter could be a blank. To make a book shorter you could run chapters on instead of a chapter ending with a half-page or a third of a page. You could start your new chapter with two or three blank lines and then start your chapter title immediately underneath that. So there were various ways you could do it. Sometimes it would be a matter of changing the typeface. You would pick one that had a wider set and then that would bump out the number of lines it would make in a paragraph, and number of lines per page and so forth. So, by using those tables which Monotype[3] published, you could do various calculations.

We had a mixture of type in the respect we worked on the point system and we also worked on the older pica system where it was Nonpareil, Brevier, Longprimer etc. So we had the two systems working in conjunction with each other, which was a wee bit of a problem. We had to be careful shall we say in when you were going to typeset something, you had to measure the typeface to make sure you were going to make a correction using the correct typeface, either the old Pica system or the point system. And it really meant duplication in some instances of the founts that we were carrying. And there was a limited range of some old wooden type which we used very very occasionally for a wee poster or something like that. It was so infinitesimal it was almost not there.

They had a reasonable range of typefaces, I would say. Bembo, Baskerville, Times New Roman, Gill Sans and Perpetua were the popular ones. They had old style, traditional, modern, Bodoni. They had a reasonable range of typefaces in a good range of sizes, from maybe six or seven point, up to maybe eighteen, twenty-four, perhaps thirty, thirty-six point.

If you were going to compare like for like with another bookshop, they were probably on a fair par with any other. Commercial companies, jobbing shops would maybe have a different range of typefaces, obviously for the type of work that they were doing. I can recall going along to Neills,[4] who were fairly close by us, and also to Oliver & Boyd to the print side, to occasionally get some type, it might ha' been lines o' type or maybe just some characters.

I can also recall borrowing matrices of some characters, and those were wee moulds of the typeface itself, of the character, which would be small brass, piece o' brass with the character incised on one end of it, and that would be fitted into the matrix case of the monotype casting machine. And it may have been a special character for a book, maybe a Tilda N or something peculiar, an umlaut or something like that, you know, something that wasnae normal. And they would fit it into the matrix case. When it was keyed by the keyboard operator it produced a spool of paper with two holes in it. When the spool was fitted to the casting machine, it was driven forward by sprocket holes at either side. It went forward and brought each character which was represented by those two holes, brought the character in the matrix case over the top of the nozzle of the melting pot, the molten composition. The lead was pumped up and that character was formed within the mould and then ejected, with all the characters and spaces to form a line and then eventually form a galley, which was made up into page form at a later date. So yes, I would say from the aspect of typefaces, Nelsons probably had a reasonable selection.

Often type was distributed back into the case again, or just dropped into a box for melting to go back into the monotype casting machines. The wooden type and the odd wee thing that cropped up was distributed back. The general average typeface in everyday sizes that were used were generally just dumped into the box for re-melting. But if you were using some of the larger display sizes, we'd never put that away for re-melting, it would have been distributed back into the case again for later use.

Oh aye, that was a time-consuming thing. Although having said that, to be fair there wasn't a lot of type that was re-distributed back into the cases because primarily most of the type for those books was coming off the monotype machines. It was just dumped into boxes for melting into ingots for recycling. But if you did have to distribute anything it was time-consuming dropping every character and spaces into their respective box. You built up a speed as you'd build up a speed for typesetting, but it was quicker to distribute than it was to typeset, because in typesetting you have to justify the lines, whereas with the distribution you didn't.

As an apprentice another laborious task was to go down to the yard and lift off the ingots that were to be fed into the monotype casting machines and give them over the boxes of type to be taken away for recycling. And generally it was two apprentices at a time who were designated to do this. You had a barrow with a wooden platform on it, a wee bogie thing, and you had to go round half the factory from the Caseroom down to this yard, which was truly no more than about thirty, forty yards away. But there were so many varying floor levels in the factory that you couldn't get down to the yard other than as I say by going round all the other departments to reach the yard.

I remember an occasion when another apprentice and I had this barrow with the wooden platform on it. There was a T-shaped metal handle on the bogie. We were going down a ramp and at the bottom of the ramp there were a couple of swing doors with porthole windows in them. We looked through the porthole windows and there was no sign of anyone coming from the opposite direction so we jumped onto this bogie, holding the metal handle between us. Foolishly, we didnae realise the doors opened in the way, so we hit those double doors and took them off their hinges! We ended up on our backs and och! I don't think we hurt ourselves but I'm sure we had sore bones and were aching. But we went away to the joiner and said, 'Look, can you do us a favour and put those doors back on their hinges before the gaffer finds out, otherwise our feet'll no touch the ground!' I'm sure there were quite a few incidents of that sort of thing that would happen, you know.

The linotype machine was there when I joined Nelsons but I think it was only about a year old at that time and they still had it when I left. I left in 1961. Generally it was the very cheap, low end of the market that the linotype machine was used for. When you looked at a typeface, if you looked at a printed page, you could detect that it was a linotype face as opposed to a monotype face, I mean, a trained person like a compositor could. Letters like 'f', where the top part, what they call the kern, overhung the body of the type. In monotype you had ligatures, an 'f' and an 'i', an 'f' and an 'l', 'ff', 'ffl', that type of thing. When the two bodies of the 'f' and the 'i' came together, the kern part of the 'f' would touch the dot above the 'i' and the kern of the 'f' would break off, and so maybe some keyboard operator would actually type an 'f' and an 'i' separately as opposed to using the ligature, and then it would break off and when you were lookin' at a printed page and you saw this broken 'f', you would realise. In fact, not only that, the ligature didn't have a dot above the 'i' — the top o' the 'f' kerned right over the 'i' and it didn't have a dot on it. So if you saw an 'f' and an 'i' together and the 'i' had a dot, you would know it wasn't a ligature. Whereas with the linotype, the 'i' had a dot on it. But it also had a different appearance, a different typographic shape to its characters than what monotype had, so if you were looking at a Times Roman linotype face, you could tell that it wasn't a monotype Times Roman face. Just one of those things that we knew. The layman would-nae know the difference, but from the aesthetic point of view, the monotype faces were beautifully designed.

We used to have wee hand-presses, for proofing something up to do a wee check on it after you'd typeset it and you were looking at it overall for, whatever, spacing, general style, checking spelling, grammar and that type of thing. You used to clean the ink off the typeface with just a rag and you used a liquid called naphtha, and it was horrible. Oh it had a horrible smell like cat's urine, really pungent! We used to put this on a cloth and wipe over the typeface and it took away the ink. Used to clean it up. But when that dried on your hands, it used to evaporate and dry and leave a white deposit on your hands. Oh, and it smelt to high doh! I'm sure I can remember coming home, and my mother making comments about this horrible smell! Oh, it ponged, hung in the air for a while. It was horrible stuff.

There was a big hand-press in the corner and then even-tually after a number of years they introduced another flatbed press with a big cylinder on it. Now, that was closer to us and when the guy that was working on the proof press was cleaning up the type there, he was liberally applying this naphtha to it. Oh, the smell was terrible!

I remember there was a Frenchman, he was one of our readers. He was actually French — we had, let me think, two

Jamaicans, two West Indian lads. They arrived at different times. One was a keyboard operator. He had a nickname, 'The Duke'. His surname was Wellington, I can't recall his proper Christian name but he was nicknamed 'The Duke'. Nice type o' lad, big handsome fellow, I would have said. He was married to a white lass. She wanted to marry him and initially he was a wee bit hesitant because of the colour difference, but eventually they got married and I think they had a successful marriage. The other lad that came across, I can't recall his name, but he was a lay preacher and he worked out on the stone and wasn't there very long. I remember talking to him. He said he'd gone to have his hair cut, sat down in the barber's seat and the chap made an attempt at it but because of the close curls that he had, hadnae been very successful. I think he'd had to leave the shop without having a full proper haircut! He had to find some other barber that would do the job for him! And then, it was during the winter time I think, we were all just talking about how cold it was, and he was saying that he was absolutely frozen right through to the bone during the night when he was in bed. So I said to him, 'What have you got in the way of bedclothes?' 'Oh,' he said, 'I've got a sheet and a blanket,' and we all burst out laughing. We said, 'A sheet and a blanket? That'll not keep you warm in our climate!' And we said, 'We've got a sheet, probably three or four blankets or three blankets anyway and maybe a big quilt or something like that.' He was quite astounded that you would need that amount of bedclothes to keep you warm but in those days there was no double-, well certainly I would say in the houses that we were living in, there was no double-glazing or any-thing to assist in keeping the house warm, probably only coal fires for when you got up in the morning. The coal fire had to have all the ashes raked out and you had to light the fire again. But he was quite a pleasant chap as well, and then we also had an Indian. He and his brother had been sent over by

44

their father who had a printing company. I'm sure it was a newspaper company over in India. And they were sent over here to learn the trade as such but they were actually working in a book workshop as opposed to a newspaper company. Their surname was Gupta. The brother seemed to be a brighter chap than the fellow we had and was at a full-time course at the Heriot-Watt, whereas the other lad wasn't. He was just working a normal day. Unless it was intentional that one maybe go down a more academic line or something, I really don't know, but yeah, pleasant enough chap to get on with.

And three Swiss fellows, I recall. Must also have had a French chap, aye, that's right. We had another French chap whom I think worked on the castors. But the three Swiss fellows they worked on the stone. They spoke German as their kind o' native language from the German side o' Switzerland. I remember they used to have wee competitions. They were making up a word, one single word from as many words as possible. I don't know if they were counting characters or counting words to make this composite word or not but there used to be competition doing that. They were quite anxious to mix and find out what the average Edinburgh person did in their leisure time, and they were okay about going to the pub for a pint. One of the journeymen was keenly interested in greyhound racing so he used to take them down to Powderhall[5], to watch the races and I suppose put a bet on the dogs down there. One of them left Nelsons at one point to do some of his national service. I think they could split their national service up into periods of six months at a time, or three months at a time. Anyway he went away back to Switzerland and he came back to visit us with his uniform on, his army uniform. He had the braid on the cap and rings on his jacket sleeves and a lanyard and such, you know. He really looked the bee's knees. So I said to him, you know, 'What, what rank are you, you know, with all this paraphernalia?' He said, 'I'm a lieutenant.' And I said, 'How in the hell can you be a lieutenant when you're only doing your national service?' It transpired that a lieutenant was the lowest rank in the Swiss army! Ah, of course he got the usual kid-ons about, 'Are you no' thinking about joining the Swiss Navy?' and so on. And of course wi' a landlocked country, it brought a wee smile to their faces.

They were journeymen. And they came over here just to improve their English and they worked on the stone and they were doing very basic work, just type corrections, but nothing, nothing exciting probably, you know. I don't know whether it'd have been a working holiday but it was a work experience to basically improve their English.

Well, they must have been there, I would have thought maybe eighteen months, something like that. They had some friends who had come over with them but they had taken up jobs in London. And when they met and tried to converse in English, they couldn't understand each other, 'cause of the different accents and colloquialisms that were being used.

So as I said, there was quite a fairly mixed batch of foreigners. I dunno if there were many English folk there, don't know of any that I can recall now that I think of it. We had one lad came in. He'd been working on a cruise liner, or a number of cruise liners over the years, producing their wee daily newspapers and menus and I suppose dance tickets, whatever you get. He was the type of guy that would have a woman in every port. Came up with a few saucy stories from time to time!

There was one guy in the department, a single fellow, a man called Willie Kerr, a wee bit of an eccentric in some ways. I don't know if he was altogether popular with everybody but he was an immensely strong chap and he used to tense his muscles, his stomach muscles, his arm muscles and so on. And he would say, 'Punch me as hard as you can now! Hit me with that mallet as hard as you can!' And he wouldnae flinch. And if you punched him, you ended up with sore knuckles. Immensely strong.

I recall we had a fifty-six pound weight, and we used to lift it at arm's length like this, with an arm out, and we used to time ourself, how long can you hold it with your arm out like this. Three, four seconds probably. Down it would go! But Willie used to lift this and throw it from hand to hand like this as if it was just a rubber ball — from hand to hand. And one day he wrapped this up in some rags and he was standing throwing it from one hand to another, and somebody came along and he said, 'Here, what weight do you think is in that?' And he threw it to the person to catch. It fell like a ton of bricks onto the floor. Could have broken the lad's toes or anything. And then of course Willie realised how foolish he had been in doing something of that nature.

But only some people I think could get on with Willie, or talk to him, have a joke with him. Other people he didnae take kindly to them. I think he used to give them short shrift. But I got on fine with Willie. I found him okay. He and the lad in charge of the casters, Jock, who was another very exceptionally strong fellow. They used to have tussles of strength. I remember Willie putting his two, these two fingers, round Jock's wrist there, like that. And Jock was a heavy-made man. He might have been about five foot ten and maybe about sixteen, seventeen stone, something like that, but not fat, he was just well-made and strong. And Willie, I don't know, it must have been a nerve or something or other that's there, I don't know. But Willie squeezed his, those two fingers, and he had Jock on his knees. Quite amazing. Just like that, aye! And he squeezed, and Big Jock went down. I've never seen it happen again. But aye, there was folk you could have good laughs with. Oh, Tommy, Tommy, Tommy, Tommy. What was Tommy's last name? I've forgotten it. Oh, I can visualise him, learner journeyman. He was a fellow that was always game for a laugh. If somebody was down in the mouth, Tommy would get them laughing again very quickly.

There was the usual banter, like a letterpress machine-man's only a comp with his brains bashed out, that sort of terminology was used and so on. And they would say the same about you. 'Och, you're a letterpress machineman wi' your brains bashed out!' I don't know if there was envy, but there was a wee bit o' a tendency for comps to have an air of, I'll not say cockiness, supremacy, superiority, but if you want to take facts, then the majority of senior managers, estimators, and the likes were former comps.

At one point when I must have been a journeyman, I took on the post of being Clerk to the Chapel. There was the Father of the Chapel and the Clerk to the Chapel, Chapel being the name for part of the trade union. The union we were part of was the Scottish Typographical Association,[6] which had two branches, one for the compositors and one for the letterpress machinemen. It was known as the STA, Scottish Typographical Association, and they used to have meetings. I think it was monthly, and we paid subs which were agreed by the union and the members. It must have been a percentage of our earnings. And it was quite, quite a high fee. I don't know what the percentage was but I can remember at one time paying seven and six a week, although I think it was collected fortnightly. And whereas other personal friends, they were maybe only paying about one and six a week to their trade union, whatever it happened to be. So in relation it was quite high. I think there were various benefits. There was sickness benefit. If you were off work, and you were off ill, you got a weekly payment of some sort. So probably the payment you were making was relevant to the benefits you were getting from it.

For example, when the printing trade went on strike in 1959, I was the senior apprentice in the Caseroom at the time. As a sixth-year apprentice I was given the same strike money as a journeyman which was five pounds a week. We were called out on strike. It wasn't an option. We were called out on strike by the union and it was a hundred per cent call-out. Money, increases in wages. I think we wanted additional holidays as well, which we never got, but whatever the settlement was, whatever increase we got, I don't think it compensated for the lost earnings for six weeks, particularly for journeymen. And whatever increase there was in earnings it must have taken them a good couple of years to recover the lost money. Albeit there was plenty of overtime going. Paid at time and a half. You could maybe take into consideration the additional overtime to what they were normally doing, but I truthfully don't think they gained a great deal out of it. When I say 'they', 'we', I was part and parcel of it.

It was a most gorgeous summer, one of the best summers I can recall that we've ever had in Edinburgh, and as a consequence, well I gave my mother five pounds a week at the time as my contribution to the housekeeping. So she continued to get her five pounds a week and I just took money out of the bank and treated it as a holiday. It certainly wasn't a holiday for journeymen who had young families. That amount of money wasn't sufficient to keep them going and it wasn't the thing to do but a lot of them had to take jobs, maybe working on farms or whatever, just to get additional income. And as a consequence, a lot of people left the trade at that point and never rejoined after the strike ended.

Certainly no-one within the Caseroom that I can recall didn't come back. But through evening classes and meeting up with folk from other companies, that was the information that came back to me. Now, as an apprentice getting that sort of money and with the weather being as it was, we all used to meet up in the playing field and we would organise five-a-side football and rounders, you know, a ball game, and various other things. We took a sandwich with us and stayed all day.

Parkside Bowling Club which was Nelsons bowling club, was adjacent to us, so we could go in there and that was my first introduction to playing bowls which I've now taken up in my later years. But my first game of bowls was as an apprentice when we were on strike. And we'd adjourn from there into the clubhouse, maybe a game of dominoes, game o' darts, game o' cards, pint o' beer. We just really treated it as a holiday, as far as apprentices were concerned.

When we went back to work, there was probably as much overtime going as you would want to work. As apprentices, working overtime wasn't particularly popular because of the hourly rate that we were being paid. And as I said earlier, over the winter months, we went to night classes three times a week, and in the summer we were expected to work overtime, and for whatever reason, I don't know, but in the Caseroom they opted to work Monday, Tuesday and Wednesday, three consecutive nights. So we were starting work at half seven in the morning, and finishing our overtime at nine o'clock at night. And by the time you came out — the pubs were shut at ten in those days! You didn't have time to go home to have a wash and a change, so if you wanted a pint o' beer, meet up with your pals, you had to go straight from work. But by the time normal finishing time on the Thursday came around, you just felt you had never been anywhere, you had been in the place for so many hours. It wasnae conducive to my social life, I know that for sure!

The wage slips in those days were quite long, they might ha' been about twelve inches long, no exaggerating. Wee narrow things about, oh we'd be lucky if they would be three quarters of an inch deep. But we used to paste these on a sheet o' paper, one below each other and we had a copy of the income tax tables, and we used to do a wee calculation. So we used to calculate if we worked a full week, our wages would be so much. We added that to the previous week's tally, worked out our income tax that we would have to pay the government. And then we would calculate it on one night's overtime, two nights' overtime, three nights' overtime, and then we'd, at some point realise, well, if we work this third night's overtime, we're gonna be working for the government. We were paying it all in tax. So we would say, 'Bugger that, I'm not doing that.' So you'd just make up some excuse, 'I've got such and such, I can only do two nights next week.' 'Cause there was no point in working for nothing. Or on some occasions we would say, 'Right, if we clock in a minute late, they'll knock off quarter of an hour's pay, and we'll save ourself a shilling in income tax', so just for devilment we did that. We worked on a Thursday to a Wednesday week. I think that was how it went. So at the last clocking in on the Wednesday, after lunch, we'd clock in a minute late. True enough, our wage slip would come through and we'd work it all out and say, 'Right, that's how it worked out.' So that was how we used to spend some of our lunch time in doing things like that! Well, you werenae doing the government, you were doing yourself a favour!

Occasionally we were asked to work with this founder's type, which had a high lead content. There must have been some health and safety agreement that whenever we were working with it, we were allowed a free pint of milk for that day. I don't know if it was a Factory Act. I'm not aware of anything specific that was highlighted in any way. Certainly there was nothing in the respect of a safety factor on the monotype machines, to prevent you being splashed by the hot metal. There wasnae a guard of any, any kind that I thought would have been adequate anyway. There was a wee dairy close by and I can recall myself and probably the next apprentice to me, who was only three months ahead of me in his apprenticeship, he and I were often sent out for milk for the people who were working with the wee, hard type. And certainly, I would say, through my apprenticeship, I had regular occasions to use the hard type and qualify for this free milk. I think there was a link with tuberculosis and lead poisoning. Whether drinking milk was of any benefit, I don't know! But I remember that aspect of it anyway.

There wasn't a hydraulic lift of any kind to lift the formes from the stone down to floor level. It was purely manual. Depending on how heavy it was, if you were daft enough, you would do it yourself. If it was too heavy, you would give someone a shout to say, 'Give me a hand to lift this down.' Some of the formes would be well over a hundredweight, but because of the bulky size you wouldnae want to try and lift one down anyway. Some of the larger ones you could manage on your own. You lifted them up a little to make sure there was nothing going to fall out o' the chase. You would lift it up on its end and you could quite easily lift it off, and you had a knack of lifting it down onto the floor.

For a long time we'd no means of conveying it from there to a rack. You used to slide it into a rack and it lay there, until the next time it had to be worked on. And then after a while, I must have been there four years anyway, before they got a wee bogie, which was maybe just a couple of inches wide by twelve inches long. This had a channel in it, into which the forme used to sit. It had wee wheels, and you just rolled this along and you could slide the forme into the rack from there. There was a tray thing, you would call it, into which you could slide the forme from the stone. That could then be turned at right angles so the forme was lying vertical, and it could be locked in that position, or probably just off the vertical, it'd be a slight angle. There must have been a hydraulic system for lifting it up and down. You could wheel it away to a printing machine for example, which might be at a different height from your stone. But we never ever had any of those.

Monotype was a composition of lead, tin and antimony. I don't know what the percentage of lead in the old type-founders hard type was, but it was very high.

For some reason or another, I don't know why, it seemed to be traditional that compositors wore white aprons. And I don't know why because with the lead in the type you got yourself black. Your fingers were black! And of course your aprons got black as well with this material you were working with. It's crazy, I don't know why we never wore black aprons! But these were taken home generally once a week and washed. They had a pocket at the front where you could keep tweezers and what we called bodkins and bits and pieces.

I think I eventually aspired to buying an overall kind of jacket, that came down to my knees as opposed to the apron that tied from round the back to the front. There were side pockets and a breast pocket where you could keep pencils and tweezers and all sorts a' things in it. I aspired to that type of coat, overall thing. But there was no compulsion, I think, to wear anything. It would have been quite nice if they'd supplied you with overalls and took them away and laundered them.

The two Miss Parks, the two sisters, I don't know what their title was but I think they were kind of personnel officers, I don't know. Aye, they were both quite nice women, couple of spinsters. Really, I thought, at my age at that time, really old-fashioned looking. They lived up near Little Road at Liberton, that direction, and I recall having to go out to their house on some errand. The foreman, Jack Breadon, said to me, 'Will you take that out to Miss Park's house?' and I remember going out to their house. But they were quite pleasant women from what I recall.

In those days there was a factory doctor who was a kind a inspectorate came round, and employees up to the age of eighteen would periodically — I don't know if it was annual, it must have been annual — go down to rooms that these Miss Parks had. From what I remember they asked you, 'How's your general health been since we last saw you?' And so on. And I think that they looked at your hands to see if there was nicotine stains. And anybody that had that was scolded for smoking and told the bad omens about it. Maybe looking for warts, bitten nails, anything like that, general health factors and so forth.

I don't know what else they asked or did, except I recall an apprentice who worked under me, he was away for a long time and when he came back I said, 'Where the hell have you been?' I said, 'You've been away for ages.' 'Oh aye,' he said, 'I'm sorry about that.' He said, 'I heard the factory doctor's in,' and he said, 'We're getting called down.' And I said, 'Well, so what? Have you been down to see the doctor?' 'No,' he said, 'Not yet.' I said, 'Well, why have you been away so long?' 'Oh,' he said, 'They examine your feet and your toes and see if you've got any problems with your feet.' And he said, 'I cannae remember when I last washed my feet!' In this yard that I mentioned earlier where lorries came in to deliver paper and the likes, there was an outside staircase leading up to gents' toilets. He said, 'I went up there and I put my foot down the toilet, and I flushed the toilet,' he said, 'I washed my feet!' 'Hell's teeth,' I thought, 'Why didn't he go and do it in a basin?' but obviously he probably wouldn't be wanting to do it in the basin with anybody else round about him!

There's some other pranks they got up to. There was this row of WCs and there were spaces, from the bottom of the door to the ground. You weren't allowed to smoke in the department so I think guys used to go up on the pretext of using the toilets and took their paper with them, the morning paper, and their fags and then sit and have a smoke. 'Cause when you went in there you could cut the air with a knife, it was so thick with cigarette smoke. I think some of the apprentices used to have a peek under the door, to recognise who was in that particular cubicle. They used to take a paper bag and fill it with water under a tap and then used to heave it over the door! The poor individual that was sitting on the toilet used to get this bucket of water over the top of them. Of course there'd be a roar and a shout and the door would open and a chase would follow on, you know.

We probably had about eight public holidays. I can't remember exactly. There were certain fixed ones like the spring holiday and the autumn holiday. We used to get a vote on which holidays were to be taken throughout the year. And I can recall working on Christmas Day. I was the only member of my household who used to go out to work on Christmas Day. Aye, but it was by choice, because that was one of the votes and it struck me as being rather strange with a predominantly female workforce, I would have thought they would have carried the vote and that they would have wanted to have Christmas Day off, particularly with the preparation of Christmas meals and the likes, you know. But the vote went in favour of working on Christmas Day, strangely enough. It sounds a kind of a heathen thing to have done!

I have relatives in the north-east of England, and as a schoolboy I remember going down there, celebrating the Christmas festive period and then coming back home for New Year where it was celebrated in similar fashion, more so, back up here at New Year time. And I think I used to find it rather strange that there was nothing exceptional happening at Christmas when I worked. That was true, nothing exceptional happened in Edinburgh at Christmas time in those days that I can recall. You just went into your work as normal, although as I say my family didn't and I was the only one out.

We did have a fairly active social life. There was a football team. There were annual dances, picnics. Dances were always something to look forward to. It was generally a dressed-up affair in dinner suits with bow ties and evening dresses for the ladies. We had used some of the better function suites with the good bands of the day. Cam Robbie and his orchestra, that type of thing. I can recall some good dances, aye. As I say, the Caseroom was a thoroughfare for staff going from one part of the offices to the other part of the offices at the far side of the building. There was a lot of staff went through and of course we used to get chatting with them, and of course you used to meet in the canteen as well, that type of thing.

I remember two journeymen chaffing me and saying, 'See you eyeing up this wee lass that comes through, we think you've got a fancy for her.' And I said, 'Do you think so?' 'Oh aye, for sure. We're sure she's got a fancy for you.' 'Aye', I says, 'Aye, okay, I'll let you think what you like.' Eventually they got to the stage, where it was coming up towards the dance and they said, 'Tell you what. If we were to buy a double ticket for the dance and put up some pocket money, some spending money, I bet you wouldnae ask that lassie to go to the dance with you.' And I said, 'Are you making me an offer, like?' Yes, of course, they were sure I wouldnae accept it. So I said, 'You're on!' They said, 'I bet you don't do it.' And I said, 'I bet I will!' I said, 'You put that offer, and I'll take you up on it.' So they did. But unknown to them, I'd been going out with the girl for about a month beforehand! So I don't think I took the money from them. I think I had to be honest and own up. Aye, as I said, they were good dances.

We decided to start up a wee kind o' social club, using the canteen premises and they were made over to us. There must have been representatives from each department or something on a wee committee. But I do remember a chap from the office, Stewart Dalgleish and myself as being two of the principal people that got the wee social club off the ground, mainly for the apprentices. We had discos and I remember we took a boat trip out to Inchcolm.[7] I can't remember how many made the trip, probably about thirty or something. We had a picnic across there.

I think it was wee bands and wee, wee groups for the dances. I've forgotten what else we did. Probably organised one or two visits to *The Scotsman* and that type o' thing. I can't remember how long that lasted. I can't remember if it was still ongoing. I think perhaps it was when I left.

Certainly there was the bowling club. It was principally their employees that were members. I don't know if they actually allowed non-employees, outsiders as such, to be associate members or not. At that time, there was a bowling league within the printing industry. That kinda fell by the wayside over the years. My own bowling club around the corner had a friendly match once a year with Parkside Bowling Club.[8] By that time it was a private club. But there were still former Nelson employees as members of it. So I used to come across former workmates. I think there was quite a good social camaraderie among the folk that worked there. As I say, there was families there, between grand-parents, parents, their children and offshoots of cousins and whatever else, you know! Brothers and sisters. So that in itself maybe helped this kind of social relationship.

I remember a couple of women laying on when I first started as a first-year apprentice but I never really got to speak to them. I remember seeing some women in the litho department but I never really got to know them either. Women in the bindery but — you kinda got past them as quickly as you could! Well, again, I was the youngest ap-prentice, and because we had fifty guys, or forty-odd guys in our department I had to serve the tea. We used to have a tea break at ten o'clock in the morning.

You went down to this wee place off the limp sewing department, it was dark, the women were working on sewing machines and such. You had to go through a door into a dark area which was fairly small and in the far wall there was a hatch, which they opened up and they passed out these big kettles o' tea. Handle up here. And I think we required two for our department. So you went back up where the men had left their mugs or cups out and you just topped them up. Eventually you took the teapots back when they were empty.

But you were told when you first joined the company, that when you went down to collect the teapots as a new apprentice, you were going to get an introduction to the bookbinder's daughter! And this conjured up all sorts of thoughts in your mind. You were dead scared to go into this wee, dark room to pick up this teapot, you know. But you passed the lassies, there were all sorts of remarks being passed at you as you were going through. I think in general they were all right, quite nice lassies. Certainly we mixed with them at the dances, you know. I would say there was quite a number married other working colleagues there.

It was good days. I suppose it could only have been about eight years or something that I was there. But I enjoyed them. I met a lot o' nice people and learnt a lot, and it set me on the road to the various jobs that I've had. I think it all stems back to my early training. The encouragement I was given by Jackie Breadon and Bobby Hogg and other foremen and other journeymen and such that I worked alongside. They encouraged you all the way and never hesitated in answering any questions that you had, or they tried to find out the answer if they didnae know themselves, you know.

Aye, it was a good place. I think it was quite a happy environment for a lot of people. As apprentices, you had a wee bit of rope to wander off to another department on some ruse, but if you had good reason to go, which might be to take a proof of something to somewhere or go into the foundry and so on, then you got the opportunity of meeting those other working colleagues which maybe you would never either meet at the canteen or a social function of some kind. You know, you would see them through your working life and you would see what they were doing and you'd be, again, curious to say, you know, 'Why are you doing this?' and 'What's it for?' and putting it into context. But the printing world's a fairly confined environment in the respect that you would meet people and they'd moved on to another company and you would meet them in different stages of your working life in different places that you go, maybe coming across them again and again.

I applied myself, and I went to my day release classes and my evening classes. Not that I was dissatisfied with being a compositor because I enjoyed the work and I've never regretted having served an apprenticeship as a compositor. There's a lot that I still carry forward to my present-day job. I'm Printing Manager for Falkirk Council, and even earlier jobs that I've had — I was Printing Manager for Lothian Regional Council and I was General Manager for Edinburgh University Students Publication Board and Sales Manager for a group of companies based in England.

In all those areas, in speaking with customers or other members of staff, my knowledge of the typographic side of printing, coupled with the little that I know about other aspects has helped. Certainly, errors, whether they be grammatical errors or whatever, in a typographical field jump out at me. You don't have to read something, it's just there, it hits you. Partly because of my training as a compositor. So I've never regretted that. I think probably the majority of administrators, maybe not so much recently where there are now courses for administrators, but maybe up to about twenty years ago, the majority of managers and administrators within printing companies were former compositors. They had to know a wee bit about every other process that followed the composing side. They had to know impositions which affected the way a sheet was going to be folded which was part of the binding operation, for example. They had that wee bit o' insight into other departments within the print field.

It was sad for Edinburgh losing such a prestigious educational publishing establishment. Somewhat of a loss. When I speak to people nowadays, the name Nelsons doesn't mean very much to them. 'Who are you talking about?' And I would say who they were and where they were located, but it doesn't mean a great deal.

Notes

1 Test took place in Psychology Department, University of Edinburgh.
2 Newbattle College, training college for adults.
3 The Monotype Corporation Ltd published guides such as *'Monotype' Keyboard Manual*, published in 1966, in collaboration with The National Committee of Monotype Users' Associations, London.
4 A & S Neill, Edinburgh.
5 Powderhall race track for racing greyhounds.
6 Scottish Typographical Association. For a history of the STA, see Scottish Typographical Association, *Scottish Typographical Association. A Fifty Years' Record, 1853–1903*, Glasgow, 1903. The STA also had a monthly periodical, *Scottish Typographical Journal*.
7 Inchcolm is one of the islands in the Firth of Forth.
8 Parkside Bowling Club was established in 1902 for Nelsons employees. The club is still located at Holyrood Park Road, Edinburgh.

ERIC MARTIN

I had relations had worked there: my grandfather and an aunt that both worked there. Grandfather had been away a long time before that. And the aunt, she'd been away a long time too. They both worked in the bindery actually. But I worked in the reproduction department. That was like when they drew the pictures, the artists drew the pictures for, like, children's books, things like that. We had to copy them, photograph them, and make the plates that went onto the machines. And they'd churn off the picture.

Well, before that I worked in Hislop and Day.[1] That was just a blockmakers. They just made the blocks. And I went to the army and when I came back from the army after three years, I went back to Hislop's. I didn't like it somehow or other. It was a tiny wee place. It was quite cramped and that, so I thought, ach well, look for some other place. And then a job in Nelsons turned up just at the right time. You had to do it through the union, you see. You just couldn't walk up and into the place and ask for a job. You had to do it through the union. So I was quite lucky it turned up just at the right time.

It so happened that the man, he had left Hislops before. I did actually know him, but at the time I didn't realise he was so high up. I knew he worked there but I didn't realise he would be giving me the interview, you see. I had worked wi' him in Hislop's for quite a while. And he went to Nelsons and got promoted quite quickly, you see. So the interview actually wasnae much of an interview, because he knew me. I had worked with him for a long time. But in these days, it wasn't

61

so much qualifications and that. It was if you'd worked with somebody and they knew how you worked and that, it was that sort a thing, you know. If they knew you could do the job that was more or less it. So that was in 1952, I think. And I was there till the very end, 1969.[2]

We were near the front. We were kind a high up. We just went straight in the main door and along a broad corridor and we went up a flight o' stairs and we were in a kind a high-up bit. Which was quite a good view. There was a bit at the back, you know. There was a kinda high building in there. But I was really quite near to the main door. Firemen used to say that was the biggest fire risk in Edinburgh was Nelsons. The whole place was lined wi' wood. All around the offices and the corridors and things. All wood. Because I think Nelsons had forests in Canada. And the firemen used to say, 'If this goes on fire, it'll go straight through the whole place in no time.'

Ours was a comparatively small department. There was three camera operators. There was three journeymen and there was one apprentice. And the retouchers, there was six retouchers, and they had an apprentice. Retouchers were kind a' artists. They worked on the plates, you know, accentuate things and a' that. One of them was an old man. He was seventy-six, Bert Japp, and he was still working there. I mean he was well past retiring age but they just kept him on. Nelsons was like that.

Old Bert Japp. A comical old character he was! He was still there when he was seventy-six, and he'd been there for, oh, I don't know how long. He had worked some place else but I think he'd been there since he was in his twenties. And this was him seventy-six. He was rejected for the army in the first war for a bad heart. And he was still workin' when he was seventy-six. When any time any o' the Nelsons or, you know, the high-ups came in, they always used to come and have a blether wi' him.

We were working in a darkroom. I mean not all the time, you had to go outside for the camera and print up your original on the board and then expose the plates. Now once you've exposed them, then you locked the door and developed them in the dark. We were very lucky. We could lock the door and we could smoke. You weren't supposed to smoke. We knew once we were in there and the door was locked, that was it.

Actually there was strictly no smoking in Nelsons. What they always did, they used to go up tae, they used to go up — the toilets were outside. There was a square inside, an empty square, open square. And there was toilets up there and they used to go in there. Oh, you really could cut the place with a knife, for smoke in it.

But anyway, old Bert, he didnae bother aboot that, and he was a heavy smoker too. Usually when somebody came up, he would be standing, and he would be smoking. Outside in the place, no, in the darkroom, and he would stand and talk to the like o' the bosses and when they come in, he would put the cigarette behind him — and he started talking to the Nelsons. And the smoke was — you could see the smoke coming out the back of him like that! Nobody ever said a word to him.

Tam Brown. Aye, he was one o' the characters, he was. When the war started, he worked in the machine room as a labourer. And he went to the Black Watch and he got his leg blown off in Italy. And when he came back, he couldnae do this labourin' job in the big machine room, so they gave him a job up beside us just as a general kind a' filing, well, there was a lot a' filing there. The negatives had to be stored away. Also books, printing, and he had this book and that. And he was a right character, a right joker, especially with this leg o' his. And anyway, one time, he must ha' been off ill or somethin', and some o' the apprentices or somebody was sent to find negatives and they looked up his book. And a lot o' the books were, you know like *The Seven Secrets*, and he'd put everything in this book o' his in the 'T's. Which was pretty useless. Everything was under 'T' because of the way they were starting with 'The', you see. Oh, they were laughing and cursin' at the same time because they couldnae find the stuff because there was so many o' the books started with 'The'. Really what he should hae done, he should hae started wi' the second word but he didnae. Oh, he was a right character, he was.

When you were just out your apprenticeship, you just did line work, which were only drawings made wi' lines, you know. And then, the next stage was black and white half-tones. You know, no colours to it. And then the sort a' top one was the colour one where you had to make all the different negatives to make the colour picture. You gradually sort a' worked your way up. Once you learned to do one, you moved onto the next.

I suppose you could learn it in a comparatively short time, but then, sometimes if there was a man up above you doing the colour work, you mibby couldn't get a chance of doing the colour work because he was there you see. And if he left or retired or something, then you would maybe move up to it, to the colour work. I suppose a year would be plenty time to learn it really.

Line work was comparatively simple, you know. You see by the time I got to Nelsons, you got films in photographic boxes, so you only loaded them onto the work of the camera, which was easy. When I first started in Hislops, 1943, we used to have to actually coat glass plates in collodion, actually make the glass plate and make them sensitive. It was actually wet when you put it in the back of the camera. You'd get glass — it was very good glass and it had to be flat. And you got this mixture of collodion with silver nitrate on it and you had to pour it on in a special shape. You dribbled it on into a circle and you had to get it to every corner, you see. And at the same time, you wanted to get the same thickness, so you had to try to get it to come right down and cover the plate and be reasonably the same thickness. That was a bit of an art on its own actually. And then by the time you'd done that, well then you put it in the baths with silver nitrate and that made it light sensitive, and then you put that plate in the back of the camera.

This was the old way. Once you'd put that into the camera and exposed it, you had to come back and then you used to have to develop it. When it was still wet, you had to bring it out and you had to put it in a vat o' cyanide, which cleared certain bits away. Then you put it into an intensifier, that was copper sulphate, put it in there. And then you had to put it in silver nitrate. I mean all this for one plate, which was unbelievable compared with what they do now.

I've had a few splashes o' cyanide in ma mouth. You know you're mibby talking to the next chap along and you didn't put the cyanide in a dish, it was a tank. And you did that just to keep it, you know, to get the fresh cyanide up or you couldn't be doing that. And bletherin' to the chap next and I know it splashed people. I mean as soon as you felt it, you just spat it oot. I suppose we shouldnae ha' been talkin', but —

You did wear overalls because these chemicals were corrosive. But I used to come back at night and my nails were all, well, through time, my nails were all brown and sore, sore too they were. Sometimes, see, you were supposed to wear gloves and that. But nobody did very much because they were awkward. Sometimes I used to have to lie on ma bed at night, put ma hand in a dish of cold water like that. The nails were all burning, burning so much. I don't know how I stuck it when I think of it.

Nelsons had done it that way, but by the time I went to Nelsons, they'd changed onto taking a flat film out the box. Well, what you had to do wi' it being a floppy flat film. You had a bit o' glass but the only reason for the glass was, you stuck the flat film onto the glass and stuck the glass in and then you just peeled it off again and put it in a dish to develop it. But that was much, much easier. Then when you developed it, the film was so much better you didn't have to put it through cyanide and silver and copper sulphate. You didn't have to do that. It was only one developer really, on the good films.

And then, they'd started trying to do away with film altogether. Well not altogether, but they were moving onto scanners. This was a thing called a clichagraph. What you did was (I never actually used the thing), you took this out in the daylight and you put your artwork there. You fixed that on the machine and at the other end of the machine was a special film kind a' stuff. And what happened was there was an electric eye and the machine went back and forward like that. Aye, back and forward like this, you see, and depending on the depth of the colour, or whether it was light or dark, it transmitted it to this wee knife, a wee blade onto this film. Where the eye was going that way, this knife wee pointer was digging out different sized holes from this film. And then they used that as the block, more or less. That's just really the start o' what all the modern scanners are. That was the very first sort a' thing, a clichagraph. There was no developer or anything connected wi' that. It was all out in the light and that. No developer or anything. That was just startin' to come in, nearer, well middle sixties, I suppose.

So I really saw it from making your own plates through the film and that through the clichagraph things up to the modern scanners. Basically it went in jumps, sort of. And when they first got the film out, it wasn't very stable, and about the register, it caused a lot o' trouble because it could shrink. Oh just a tiny wee bit of it was enough to put the register out. So we had to struggle wi' that for a while and then eventually they got it on a better base, where it didn't stretch, although it was still the same emulsion. So that helped a bit. And it was like that a long time till they started this clichagraph thing, you see. And that wasn't film, it was a kind a' brittle, kind of almost a plastic sort a' stuff, you know. Although it was coated with this other thing, it was an orange kind a' coating and the blade actually dug the wee bits out of the orange coating.

You see, people don't realise that coloured pictures, they're made up of thousands o' wee dots and it depended on what quality the work was how many dots there was to the square inch. Like newspapers were just rough things. There was sixty-five dots along one side of a square inch, but for good-class work it could go away up to two hundred dots. What you did was, there was a big round glass screen. And there was lines on one way on each one and then the two glass screens were joined together. Tightly joined. Glued together. But I mean that was some special kind a' glue. And when the light from the camera came through this thing onto the negative, it put these tiny wee dots as well, you see. They had to have the dots to get the different shades. You'd have a different screen for each one. Sixty-five and all the way, sixty-five, eighty-five, hundred, hundred and twenty —

Newspapers, they were about sixty-five. They were rough, you know. But you see we had to make these dots a certain size. Depended on the exposure we gave it, you know. If we made the dot and the white, made it the wrong size, it wouldn't a' looked white, it would a' looked a kind of an in between colour. But if we made too big a dot in the black, it wouldnae o' looked black. So it wasn't just one exposure you put on to get negatives. There was three. Just a general kind o' a main exposure, then an extra one to give it a bit more fuller white. And another one tae make the wee dot hard.

Even after years and years you were quite often wrong because it was so hard to judge it really, you know. It was really only experience. That when you looked at it, like that wee picture up there where it's a baby, you know it's not really white and it's no' really black. Well that would be a different exposure altogether fae somethin' that was really black and white. But it was just experience really.

There was quite a lot of mistakes, right enough. That was one thing about the old way, when you made your plates. They were only glass really so if you made a mistake, it could be scrubbed off and coated again. But with these films it was a bit of a slip, you know. They were pretty expensive. One place I worked where you needed four plates for the colour set and the boss only gave you five. You were allowed one mistake, and if there was more than one mistake you had to go and ask him for another, you know, more plate which wasn't very nice. They weren't happy about it at all.

You'd have a different screen for each one. Oh they were very, very expensive! When you started working on them, they used to say to you, 'If you drop that, just put your coat on and walk out.' I never ever saw one dropped. The last one that I used in Nelsons, this was a big camera, it cost twelve thousand away back in 1958 or something. The actual screen was round, and the idea was you turned it for each different plate so as that these dots didn't clash, you know. Well, that one, it was very, very thin and that cost seven hundred pound, away back then.

Well, the wages then were about, oh I don't know, somewhere about twenty-five pound or something like that. A week's wages about twenty-five pound and this thing was seven hundred. And you didn't always keep the screen. If you were doing line work, you didn't need the screen so you had to take it out and put it in a big box. And when you took it out, you could feel it bending. You could. It was so thin and so big, you could actually feel it bending. And I used that thing for years. And one day, somebody from the office came in and they said, they knew nothing about camera or whatever, just from the office. It was an accountant or something like that. And he came and he says to me, 'Have you got a half-tone screen here?' I says, 'Aha.' He says, 'Could I see it?' I say, 'That's it under there.' He says, 'You know that part there is seven hundred pound.' He says, 'You know that costs seven hundred pound and it's not under our insurance.' And I'd been using it for years. It wasn't under their insured. They had other things but somehow or other they missed that out.

Aye, you see the camera had lenses and that, but they were more a fixture in the camera. This thing went out and in and somehow or other it got left out o' their counts, you see. Good job I didny know that, 'cause I was never happy using that thing because it bent.

So what you did, you made up one negative with a colour filter. Then you made another one, blue, red, green, yellow. You made the negatives through these filters. Different negatives. And that brought up, you know, different parts o' the picture and then there was other men, retouchers, they had to accentuate the colours and that.

Say they had one of the plates off the colour set. These wee dots on top o' it. They were very important. Well, we could only get them to within reasonable sizes. What they had to do, theirs was a hard job too, they had to alter the dots. Say on the yellow plate for some reason we hadnae made it just right, what they would have to do, they had to paint out the bits that weren't yellow. And they had to actually etch the dots, to try and make them nearer to their proper colour. See, you got colour, all the colours aren't just red, yellow, blue. They're in between colours. So what they were doing as well, well they were combining say a red dot and a yellow dot off the yellow plate, say to make an orange. And if we hadnae got the dots right, they had to etch the red dot, the red plate and the yellow plate so as when they went on top of each other, these dots made an orange.

They had books that showed you, ah, well the dots were called in percentage sizes, you know. Right fae a five per cent dot right up to solid. And say you had an orange might be a sixty per cent red and a twenty per cent yellow. That weren't really my job that and I don't know what the percentage were really, but that's how they worked and they had to make these dots on each plate to the proper size so as that when they were on top o' each other you got the in between colours. Difficult job.

Oh, they had a lot o' artwork. They had to paint round some, well a kind of dye stuff that wouldn't etch and when once they'd painted it all out, they etched them. They etched them down so far and then when they got them to the right size they wiped the dye stuff off and protected it from the edge. And then they would mibby have to do another bit and etch the dot to a different size because it would be a different shade o' orange. Terrible job, actually.

Maps were the hardest thing to do. Sheer size was part of it. It's difficult, I suppose, when you don't know anything about it, but you know you've got railway lines and roads and towns and all that. And you make a different negative for different bits and then they all had to be combined onto one negative. So the maps were harder. They were hard.

It took a retoucher about — Well, it would take us about maybe four hours to make the plates. The negatives, when I say plates I'm meaning negatives. And might be in a couple o' days or maybe more to make one picture, one coloured picture. Oh, it was very labour intensive.

And in the end you made special metal plates that were on wooden blocks, one for each colour. Then when they put them on the machine, they printed, say a red one, blue one, all on top o' each other so you finished up with a normal coloured picture. But then it was more complicated than that because these pictures were all made wi' dots all over them, to allow for the different shade. So each colour had to be twisted so many angles, partly because if you did it all at the same angle, you'd get a great big rotten pattern on the

70

thing. It's very difficult to explain really, but it was quite hard.

Sometimes when you had to combine them there was always a register mark. You know, a cross at the top and the bottom. And sometimes what you had to do in the dark, well not a dark room, a red light, you used to mark a distinct chinograph on the unexposed film. Put a circle and that's where you put the cross of the register mark, then you exposed it. And you didn't develop the whole thing. You just put a wee drop developer on a paintbrush and dabbed it on the register mark and the register mark came up, you see. And then you could fit the next one just to that register mark. And then the next colour as well and then develop the whole lot at one time at the end.

With workin' in a red light, it was quite hard. 'Course it wasn't all just coloured pictures. There was lots o' things. Well not so much in Nelsons. It was mostly all kind o' children's books, story books and things like that. And cookbooks, like bibles and *Treasure Island* and stuff like that. That was mostly Nelsons work.

Where I was, this big camera was one o' their showpieces too, this big clinch camera. This thing cost twelve thousand. Weighed a ton and a ha'. And everybody came there. In fact, what was his name? President o' Kenya. Kenyatta, President Kenyatta, that was him.[3] And this day, there was about nine o' them come in, all African women wae these fancy African dresses. They didn't have a clue what they were lookin' at really —

And this was President Kenyatta's wife and her sister and that come. And oh aye, we used to get lots and lots o' them comin' round. And you knew that they didnae ha' an interest in what they were looking at, you know. An' some of them that would come in, you'd see that they were coming or gettin' shown round and that, and you played off whether they were really interested or no'. And some o' them, I used to say to them, 'Do you know anything about this at all?' I said, 'It's complicated.' And well, I'd be standing talking at them and they didn't have a clue what I was talking about. I asked them first. I said, 'Do you know anything about this,' sort a', you know, general kind o' thing. And most o' them said, 'No, no, I haven't the faintest idea.' I just thingied, still about the camera, the weight or whatever, the size, and all this stuff.

Different departments had different coloured overalls, so as if you were in a department wae a green overall and a' the rest had yellow overalls, you stuck out, you know. 'What was he doin' in there?' But, as I say, I never really had any much need to go to other departments.

Well you did have somethin' of the sort with the department that came immediately after you. You did have kind o' connections with them. And the plate-making was the next one to our, so we kind o' knew them alright but, say, we couldnae do their work in there. Oh they would, somebody would wander in and, sort of say, 'Have you got some such a job here?' And we would say, this was sort o' just unofficially between us asking if any o' these were ready sort o' thing, you know. And you would tell them it.

But I don't know if it's things seemed to change or — there was bad feeling. Well I don't know if you'd call it bad feeling, but there seemed to be an awful lot o' pressure went on in the printing industry compared to what it used to be, you know. Part o' the reason was, well, literally at the end, you'd be doin' somethin' or other and they would say, 'Are you finished wi' that?' or something. And you'd say, 'Oh no, it's a hard job. Not be ready for a while yet.' And they'd say, 'You know, a machine's waitin' on that. Five hundred pound an hour.' You see, the big printing machines were so expensive, you know. Half a million, a million, two million. And what they called the down-time, was waitin' time. If they didn't actually have a plate to go on, soon as they'd finished one job, they were standing doin' nothin' and this was costin'

1. Group of ex-Nelson employees, Abden House, Edinburgh, December 1998. Back row, left to right: John McDonald, Jack Osborne, Bill Reid, Robert Sinclair. W F Valentine behind Bill Reid. Middle row, left to right: Jimmy Cuthbert, Jackie Breadon, Andy Anderson. Front row: Alex McQuire. Photo: Helen Clark, City of Edinburgh Museums, 956/5; SAPPHIRE, 1999/125.

2. Drew McFarlane, Monotype keyboard operator, late 1950s.
SAPPHIRE, 1999/77.

3. Eric Martin, camera operator. SAPPHIRE, 1999/77.

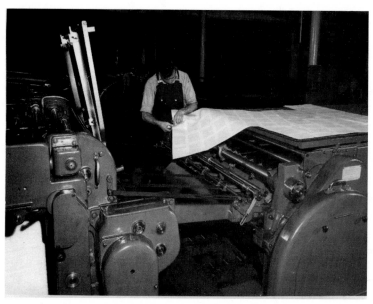

4. At the printing Press, Nelson's. SAPPHIRE, 1999/77.

5. Loading books for distribution, wareroom. SAPPHIRE, 1999/77.

6. Nelson's football team. Back Row, left to right: Jimmy Ford, George Hursh, Laurie Aitken, Rab Reid, George Wilson, Stevie Lawson, John McDonald, Andy Anderson. Front row: Alec Robertson, Fraser Renton, Don Lawrence, Gordon Payne, Douglas Downie. SAPPHIRE, 1998/38.

7. Group of workers at Flannel dance. Left to right: Jackie White, Davie Ross, John McDonald, Alec Dunny, Kenny Molart. SAPPHIRE, 1998/28.

8. Group of workers on annual trip. Back row, left to right: (?), (?), Jackie White, Davie Ross, Duggie Downie, Mary McDonald. Front row, left to right: Margo Fulton, Tommy Steedman, (?), Mae Smythe, (?), (?).

five hundred pound an hour, you see. So you were gettin' pushed. And if you were pushed and made a mistake, then you were worse off. You know our kind of job wasnae this, a job that you could hurry, you know.

I mean you used to see a factory inspector in Nelsons every few months. I remember my grandfather tellin' me there was a man in Nelsons when he was there and he got all his fingers cut off in the guillotine. But no' his thumbs. All his fingers. You know, they shoved the big piles through the guillotine and come down and cut his fingers, so maybe that had somethin' why the inspectors came so quick.[4] I don't know.

They never said very much to you. Oh well, they used to look for stuff like if there was guards on guillotines, or poisons, where was it — like cyanide was a poison. You know, they used to look around — and poison bottles. And och, they were always lookin' for fire extinguishers and things like that, you know.

Aye, well, I think we kind a' thought we were the élite. We were looked upon as kind o' snobby. 'Cause we did the shorter hours and better wages and things. Oh, maybe about an hour and a half a week or somethin' like that. Well, remember at one time, we got away at quarter to five and they got away quarter past five, something like that. But it all added up, you know. Over the days, you know.

That was where the élite came in. We never worked on Saturdays where all the rest did. Because, even when I started my time, I never worked on a Saturday. I never ever worked on a Saturday, unless it was somethin' urgent, overtime you know. Where all the rest o' 'em, it was just normal, Saturday, till about twelve or one o'clock or somethin' on a Saturday, but we never. Oh, we used to get some remarks, you know. 'Oh, it's alright for you lot, no Saturdays.' But overall there was a big difference in the amount of hours worked. I mean, for a start, there was about four hours on the Saturday, and there was about another hour and a half on the ordinary days, you know. There must have been a difference of about five or six hours in ma working week.

When I started, as I say, I didn't work on a Saturday, but I finished work at twelve minutes to six. Eight to twelve minutes to six. I think that was because it was a forty-two hour week. And then, quite soon after that, they dropped it to the forty-hour week, but for the rest it would be somewhere about forty-eight.

I remember something must have happened because I remember when we went out, we used to go out on our own, whatever time we went away. We went away before the rest. And then I remember later all of them goin' out at the same time. So they must hae caught up on us there, they must have done. I remember that now, that it seemed funny, twenty o' us goin' out and all the rest still workin'. We always started at the same time, but you got away earlier at times. We went out the side door. Where the main door was, there was a big long corridor went along, and when you got up to the end o' that corridor, there was this big open courtyard. And, that courtyard, a door went out to the left which took you oot into Parkside Terrace.

I was never very keen on overtime. In fact, for two or three years, I worked from eight to eight, Monday, Tuesday, Wednesday. For a couple o' years because it was so busy. And that was a long time, eight to eight, you know. It must have been '63, '65, so middle sixties that was. Oh aye, it was busy. We never hung about doin' nothing. There was always work there, you know. Always. I mean, I've worked, been in other places where, maybe there have been spells where you hung about for weeks doing very little. Waddies was like that for a wee while,[5] but I can never remember running out of work in Nelsons, never. You see I think they were the kind o' books like *Treasure Island* and these sort of things. I think that if they ever did get a bit short, what they did was they just printed some more o' *Treasure Island* or something like that.

These kind o' books there's always a demand for. I'm sure that's what they did. I can never ever remember goin' into no work in Nelsons.

Other places you'd get seasonal work when the festival was on or an election's on, things like that. But no, Nelsons just seemed to hold, just steady the whole time. You couldnae say that it was busier this year, or that time o' year — But the festival and elections, they *were* busy in other places.

They all had job numbers. But then you had to read dockets of course, you know you had to, of what you were doing. You had to write that all the time. It was all divided out into eight to nine, nine till ten, ten till eleven. And you had to write down the number o' the job and the name of the job, and stretch it over nine o'clock to one o'clock or however long it had taken you to do. It'd go to the accountants somewhere, I suppose. But, I don't know where actually they went. I mean, they were just collected every week — it was a weekly thing, you know. The foreman just took them away and away they went to the office, but which exact bit o' the office they went to, I don't know.

You could come in at two minutes past eight and that was alright. And after that, the ink on the clock changed to red, and that took their attention to the fact that you were late. And well, you got it deducted right enough. There was a chap. I can't remember who he was. I can't remember what he looked like. He was always late. And he'd ha' a wee stamp made. It was somethin' like, two minutes past eight or one minute past eight. And when he came in at twenty past or somethin', he stamped it wi' this wee stamp. They caught him in the end and he was oot the door immediately. That very same day, he was gone.

Wages. Weekly. Aye. In a wee tin box and we could hardly get them out. A wee tin box, about not much bigger than an egg-cup. And it was, half of it, you know, the top? Half of it was covered in wi' a bit o' metal and the money was all stuffed into this thing. It was quite easy to stuff it in — but it took us ages to get it out. Oh, I remember that. I don't know why they did that. Eventually it went to envelopes.

The clerkess from the office, she came around wi' it on the Friday. She came round individually. Handed them oot. I don't know how they gave the tin back. Sometime it took five minutes to get. Aye, I think you just gave it back to her. While she was goin' round, you emptied it and handed it back to her. Because it was always half past four on a Friday. And there was always somebody had the wrong thing, you know. So they had to run away back. 'Cause it was, as far as I know everybody got paid weekly. I mean there was no bank things or anything like that. Most paid straight into the bank. I suppose some o' the staff, I mean the foreman might ha' monthly, but — nine tenths o' the people would be gettin' this wee tin.

Oh, I thought our wages was reasonable. When I started it was thirteen shillings a week. Aye, thirteen shillings. Not that there seemed to be much bother about your wage. But o' course, it was kind a' set by the unions. You know, there was a minimum wage the unions said you had to get. But there was such a thing as you got a bit extra wage as I was saying for linework, half-tone or colour. You got extra for that. And there was such a thing as merit money. I mean they could give you more if they wanted. Say that they had to give you twenty pound, well all the ones that were there a while or better work, they offered merit money. I mean, it's still in twenty, twenty-three or twenty-five. It was like extra for being a good worker or you know, being there a long time. Well, it wasnae so much a long time, because I mean there were ones that had been there a long time that didnae get merit money. But it was mainly for being a good worker. But nobody ever knew what anybody else had got really, you know. Well, they knew, you always knew who was the best paying but not by how much. I think more or less everybody got more than the absolute minimum you know, but one or two got a fair amount more.

The foremen were all right at Nelsons. Mr Maxwell. He was, oh he'd be in his fifties when I went there. But then, the next one came, was a much younger man. I think this was Hopewell tryin' to smarten the place up a bit, you know. Must a' thought younger men would be better. But I forget where he came from. But he came from somewhere else right into the foreman's job. He was a nice chap, he was too.

But ours wasn't really big enough. No. But they did have under-gaffers. Well, I used to have to do it sometimes. When the foreman was off, I did it three times. The bigger departments did have under-gaffers, right enough. More or less, with our smaller one, because if he was off it was just kind o' worked between us, more or less, you know. David Merrilees would be the one. He was the oldest, he'd had the most experience. He used to take it at first when Mr Marshall was off.

Our union weren't on that strike. It would be the '59 strike. We were the only ones, I think, that weren't on that strike. We were the only ones in the place because our union was different, you see. Our union was sort o' élite at the time. SLADE, Society o' Lithographic Artists, Designers and Engravers, that was it. So, we had shorter hours than the rest o' them and better wages. Even if you went on shift work, we got better pay than the other unions. So our union didn't go on strike then. We were going out and in the door and the rest were standing in pickets outside.

If we'd a' went on strike, we would ha' been going on strike against something we'd already got. Oh, I can remember the managers and the bosses and the directors running around pushing barrows and things like that. 'Cause they, you see, they couldnae ask us to do their work. That would a' been a different story. As long as we were doing our own work, that was all right. If the firm had asked us to do somebody else's

77

type o' work, that would ha' been a different story but we didn't. We couldn't ha' done it anyway. Wouldn't have known what to do. We couldn't have been a bookbinder, you know. Ah, but the bosses were trying to do things, no' that they made a job of it really. I can never remember much in the way of the chapels in Nelsons. That was pretty peaceful, in Nelsons, apart from that strike.

Apprentices were sent for half-tone dots and sent for a rubber hammer and things like that, you know. And then of course, say you sent them for half-tone dots, the man you sent them to, he knew what was goin' on of course, and he says, 'Oh, I've not, I havenae got any just now. You'll need to go along there to that other place and ask him there.' And he was going round the whole place for hours, you know. Everbody knew what was goin' on so they just sent him to somebody else. So, we'd all just, 'Oh no, we've no' got any, we've run out o' them. Try Charlie along there.' Then the poor lad was goin' round aboot for -

I remember once, this chap, he was very fond o' Oxos. Oxo cubes. And he had them every morning. He used to put them in and, you know, break it up. There was wood for mountin' the blocks on and they got a bit and they cut it to exactly the size o' an Oxo cube and they stained it to look the same and then wrapped it up in a bit o' paper. And it looked the real thing right enough. And he put it in his cup and he started, you know, trying to break it up with a spoon. And saying the thing wouldn't go down, you know. And he went on for ages. Oh he couldnae understand. Oh he lost his rag wi' the thing eventually and he picked it up. He picked it up to throw it, funny Oxo cube and it dawned on him, eventually.

I'm sure in my grandfather's time there was a thousand [workers]. I'm sure there was. But now that would be going back a bit now because he died when I was in the army. He died in 1947. So somewhere in the 1930s, it was round about a thousand. And then there was a time when there was a lot o' short time as well. That must have been in the thirties. The thing was, they didn't sack them. They worked, you know, somebody was in for a week and then they were off and somebody else came in for a week. Well, I'm saying a week but it might ha' been a month or whatever, you know. But they did no' actually sack them. They kept them goin'.

Nelsons used to have a row o' tenements too, you know, for the workers. You know where Hope Park is? You know Hope Park? And you know if you go down as if you were going to the Meadows? There's a crossroads. The houses go down just across from where the Meadows start. Well, if you turn along right there at the crossroads and then you go along maybe a hundred yards, or a couple o' hundred yard, you turn right again. And there's a dead-end street wi' tenements on either side. I'm sure that belonged to Nelsons workers at one time, away back. I don't know what the name o' that street is. It's off Buccleuch Street. When they worked in Nelsons they got one of these houses to rent. And when that stopped, I don't remember, 'cause grandfather lived in Causewayside but it wasn't a Nelsons house.

If you said you worked in Nelsons, you know, like if you went to the building society or something, they said that was reckoned to be one o' Edinburgh's best places. People, I would say, were kind a', were quite proud to say they worked in Nelsons.

I tell you one thing they used to do. If you were working on something or other and you saw a mistake in it, you got something for it. Fifty pence or a pound, if you saw a mistake. Which was a fair amount when the wage would be aboot, I don' know, fifteen pound or so. But I got it a couple o' times. I was doin' a frontispiece for an astronomy book. The moon going round, the moon going round the earth, and I was interested in astronomy, and I thought, 'That's no' right. Can't be right.' It was a diagram like, and I said to whoever, 'That's wrong. I'm sure it's wrong.' So he went away an' he saw about it, and seemingly there was quite a bit o' argument about it before they found out. Nobody knew for sure whether it was right. But anyway they took it away to somewhere, and they come back and I got fifty pence for it. But, it was quite good. You know, I've seen people in other places seen something wrang and, 'Ach, I'll no' bother'.

One good thing they had was an annual kind o' sale, you know, books that hadn't sold. And you could go down and get them for practically nothing, the books that hadnae sold as well as some other ones. It wouldn't be not sold, it would be damaged copy. But you had to look hard to find the damage, you know. You got encyclopaedias and things for very little. Maybe because one of them had got damaged or something. I used to buy books. I liked reading. They used to say, 'Alright, your department can go on Tuesday afternoon' or something, and the other department go on Wednesday morning. There was quite a lot o' them, aye. 'Cause you know sometimes on a printing machine or somethin', if something goes a lot wrong, quite a lot can run through and get damaged before they can see it or stop it. So you might have quite a few hundred books lying about that you couldnae sell but there was nothing really wrong wi' them. Aye, there was quite a demand for the annual sale.

Subscriptions. Oh, they could be quite large for people that were leaving but it all depends if they were liked or not really. Well, some of the bigger departments, these ones where there's a lot o' girls an' that in it were gettin' married and things like that, they used to put away so much away every week I think. I think that's what they did. No' very much, just a shilling or two. We just used to, I mean we used to put a fair amount. You know away back then a fair amount would be five shillings, you know.

But what finished Nelsons off in the end was, there was a man, I'm not sure if this is right, Lord Thomson of Fleet? He owned *The Scotsman* at that time. The atmosphere, it did start to change. It definitely did. Lord Thomson, he used to come round and he would just stand and like he would just look at you sort a' and then he would give you a wee nod and then wander away'. He took it over, but I think I'm right in saying, he didn't take it over for very long before he sold it to the British Printing Corporation.

This was one o' the things that made everybody wonder, when the British Printing Corporation took over, they officially took over on a Thursday or something like that. I was up in the loft. I was sent up. Now, well there was a lot of very old stuff and there was a room wae the more recent stuff. And I was sent up there to try and kind a' sort them out and see what was there and all this. And the reason why it was the British Printing Corporation wanted all the reasonably recent negatives sent to, I think it was Oxford or somewhere. And obviously, everybody thought, 'What do they want all that for?' Obviously what they were wantin', they wanted all the negatives and they were going to send them to their own places. And their other places were in the south of England. And they were going to use them to print in their own factory, and they just wanted to shut Nelsons, and that's what happened. But they just more or less took what they wanted out o' Nelsons and then they got rid o' it to this Oxleys place. You see, an awful lot o' these negatives, as I say, it was a goldmine for a printing house. Schoolbooks. Maths books and English books. Just stories. There were a' these British ones and all these African countries. And what happened was, every year, they came back for a reprint. And all they had to do was change 1962 to read the new thing, to imprint, sixty-two, and change it to sixty-three. And that's all they had to do, just a few minutes' work, and then they printed the whole thousand, thousands of books again. Which was really costin' them very little because the main work would be done.

Oh, everybody was shocked. They really were shocked. Because it had gone along a long time with the Nelsons, you know. Until grandfather, and father and son-in-law. And when this news came that they'd sold it, oh aye, it was really really a shock, it was like. And people couldnae believe it. They thought it would never happen. It'd gone on for so long under the Nelsons.

They went, starting going in dribs and drabs. We were amongst the last to go. And even in certain departments some went away before others, you know. Some of them were very very lucky too. Was it the readers or the bookbinders? Some o' them were actually made redundant from Nelsons and, after things got kind a' settled down in Morrison & Gibbs[6] and Johnsons,[7] they decided they needed some more people. So they took them back on again. So they'd a' got their redundancy, and they got their job back. Where others just went straight — you know, you didnae lose anything, but just like continued.

Although there was a bit o' a row about it when they left. People reckoned that they, everybody should have got re-dundancy money, I think. Because it had been shut down and taken over by another owner. But they wouldnae have that. Course they were hard up, this Oxleys. They got round it some way. They said, they'd lend us a week's wages or some — you see, there was lyin' time to do wi' Nelson. You know how you didn't get paid the first week you went, but when you did leave, you got two weeks' wages. And there was quite a big row about that. This, they were saying about it to this Oxleys group, 'But you are another firm. Nelsons is finished. We're redundant.'

And they said, 'Oh no you're no', oh there's some financial way that they did it. They said something about, 'Oh we will lend you a week's wages or somethin'. But then you couldnae, you werenae in the whatever way of it. You couldnae say, 'Oh, I don't want a loan o' a week's wages. I want —'. Well, they got away wi' it in the end so we just changed right, oh aye.

But it was funny walking into a place, when we walked into

Johnsons. And we walked in and there was quite a fair bit o' equipment there as it was. There was three cameras there, and oh, half a dozen retouchers, two or three oper — we were in and all these chaps were there and we were going in as well. I could have just stood about for, oh, ages. And then, what they did was that they started shifts, you know to spread it out. But even that wasnae all that very much better because then there wasnae enough work to go around, you know. I don't know what happened to that place in the end.

I remember it was a sorry-looking sight when it was closed down, it really was. Because after I was away, in Easter Road or wherever I was, I got this message that I had to go back up to Nelsons. This was quite a few weeks after it had closed down. And what had happened, they'd taken this big camera in bits, down to bits, and it was going to India of all places! And nobody knew which bit was which. So I got sent back up to write, 'This is the filter, this is the screen-gear,' and all this and put wee labels on all the bits. And when I went up I couldn't believe it, because they had been taking the big printing machines away, and they'd knocked down walls and — It was like a bomb had hit it! Big walls wi' no other way o' getting the things out, so they knocked the walls down. And it was, oh it was really terrible. It was quite a sad sight, it was really. There was nobody else left in the place. I was wandering about masel'. Just, well, I mean it looked so bad, I thought, 'Am I the only one in here?'. And when I went and looked, I saw one or two doing kind a' jobs something like me, just putting labels on things. And I thought, 'Oh dear'.

'Cause I didnae expect it to be like that, you know. I knew they were taking the machine out, but I didnae think that they'd actually knocked the walls down and taking them out in big bits. And now when I got up to our bit, I see our camera was, well there were two cameras actually, but this big one was all lying in bits. Some engineer had taken it to bits but then as it was going to India, they had to put it back thegether again. Funny place for it to finish up in the end. Mmm. It was a big shock in the end.

'Cause I can remember, the funny thing not that awful long before things started tae go wrong a bit — Somebody, somebody says, 'How long do you think Nelsons'll be standing here like this?' Just a daft sort a' question, you know. Just amongst ourself. And ah, och, I don't know, I think the lowest figure was about thirty years, you know, and they went up to two hundred! Little did they know it was gone in about three. 'Cause it was just that nobody ever thought it would go like that.

I'd say Nelsons was the best place I ever worked — in the beginning, but as it came on nearer the end, things started to change, you know. Aye, Nelsons without a doubt was the best place. 'Cause it was fairly easy-oasy, you were pretty well much left to get on wi' it yerself, you didnae ha' people comin' chasin' you the whole time. They wanted quality, you know, so you got time to do the job properly.

They kind a' trusted you in a way. You know, they werenae on your back all of the time to do this or hurry up or — In fact, this Robert Marshall, I'd only been there a few days. And he brought me a job to do, and it was just simple linework, see, nothing very difficult at all. And he says to me, he says, 'Now, this job is in a big hurry.' It was the second day I was there. And he says, 'This job's in a big hurry.' And I said, 'Oh, well um, when do you want it for?' And he says, 'Well, I'll have to have it for Thursday afternoon.' Thursday afternoon! I'll have it ready for tonight! To me it was about mibby four hours' work, and he was giving me Tuesday, Wednesday and Thursday to do it and it was in a big hurry. But as I say, you had to be right, you know. Some places, they'd ha' asked you to hurry it and they shut their eyes to less than perfection, but no, Nelsons, they wanted it right.

I was going to leave once and they were pretty decent wae

me. See, I had my wife and the three o' them. Well, there wasnae three of them then but two of them. And this head retouchin' man come to me one day and he says — He'd been around a lot, worked in England and that. Although he hadn't been at Nelsons for a good while and he come to me one day and I didnae really have a house, you see. And he says to me, 'There's a man I know that's going to start up a business in Inverness.' And he says, 'He wants me to go but he needs a camera operator as well.' He says, 'Would you be ready to go?' 'I don't think so.' He says, 'You would get a house.' And I says, 'A house?' He says, 'Aye.' I said, 'Couldnae.' He says, 'Oh,' he says, 'They're getting some fae the Corporation because they're opening up this industrial bit up there.' I said, 'Oh well, that would be worth thinking' — no' that I was really wanting to leave Nelsons but for the sake o' the house, I thought about it. So I says, 'Alright then. Where is it?' Dixon's postcards, it was. So I gave in my notice. And I got called up to the big fancy office, Managing Director, and he says, 'I hear you gave in your notice.' I says, 'Mhm.' He says, 'Why?' And I says, 'Well,' I says, 'It's not that I'm really wanting to go.' I says, 'It's 'cause there's a house wi' the job.' He says, 'Oh.' He says, 'Well, I'll get back to you, I'll come back to you.' So he came back to me and he says, 'We'll give you the deposit for the house if you stay.' So that showed the kind a' decent firm it was, you know.

I had to pay them it back, but over, och, a long time, you know. I mean I didnae have any other way at that time. It wasnae easy to buy a house back in the sixties. So they gave me enough for the deposit and I paid it back over about four years, I think it was. Which was pretty decent of them really. I suppose that's how I always have a soft side for Nelsons as well, you know.

Thomas Nelson and Sons

Notes

1 Hislop & Day Ltd, 9 Albany Street, Edinburgh.

2 Nelsons closed in November 1968.

3 Nelsons published President Kenyatta's autobiography. The firm had strong African connections. Its South African branch was formed into a registered company in June 1962; trading relationships had been in existence since around 1910. The firm also had important links with Nigeria and East Africa. In Nigeria, a branch was formed in Apaca, Lagos, in 1961; trading commenced in February 1962. In East Africa, the company was registered in Nairobi on 8 October 1963.

4 The accident happened to Willie Allison, a guillotine operator in the bindery. He continued to work in Nelsons after the accident.

5 Waddie & Co Ltd, St Stephen's Works, Slateford Road, Edinburgh.

6 Morrison and Gibb was located at Tanfield Works, Canonmills, Edinburgh. The British Printing Corporation which had taken over Nelsons from the Thomson Organisation, had wanted to streamline its plants, all of which were located in the South of England. However, it was found that Nelsons could not be integrated with them. However, Nelsons could be integrated into the firm Morrison & Gibb which wanted to expand lithographic operations. The Nelson business was gradually merged with its own. Much of the machinery was transferred to the Tanfield Works, as also stocks of paper, plates and work in progress, together with the management, sales and printing staff. The buildings were vacated, and during the Commonwealth Games in Edinburgh, they were used as a security headquarters. They were subsequently demolished and redeveloped. The headquarters of Scottish Widows now stands on the site of the former printing works.

7 W. & A. K. Johnson.

BILL REID

I started in Nelsons when I was fifteen years of age. Of course, at that time you left school at fifteen. And there was none of this sixteen business. Actually I left when I was fourteen 'cause I wasn't fifteen till the summer holidays. The old adage was, 'Get a trade, son, and you'll never be out of a job.' That was your father's thinking in those days. I'm talking about 1948, '49, round about that era. You're either a painter, a plumber or somethin', a joiner, or — 'Get a good trade.' And of course at that time the printing trade was *the* trade in Nelsons. I started fancyin' off bein' a plumber, a painter for some reason or other and then I thought, no, no, and then I said, 'Well, the printing trade.'

It was Nelsons I was considered for. And it was Nelsons that took me on initially. It wasn't a kind of a pool arrangement or anything. You were designated a company. I lived that side of the town, so Nelsons was one of the nearest, apart from Oliver & Boyds. They had a really good reputation. You know, your folks said, 'Oh, he's going into Nelsons, aye, it's a good place.' And I think you just gravitated towards it rather than actually asked.

And in actual fact in those days, it's like the shipyards, you had to have somebody to speak for you. I mean fathers got their sons in, or uncles got their nephews in and that kind a' thing. I was very lucky because a cousin of mine was union steward for the lithographers, and he was able to get me the forms and able to get me into the entrance exam. And of course you had a very serious entrance exam to pass in those days. It was for colour-blindness, deafness and all sorts of things, and plus there was a sort of a IQ test as well. I'm not sure how they judged that, but there was a kind of a multiple-choice question paper, you know, '2, 4, 6, 8, what's the next number?' kind of thing. So once you satisfied them in that you were compos mentis, you got into the trade, you never got in right away because in actual fact what happened, there was a very strict rota for apprentices. It was one apprentice for three journeymen tradesmen, two apprentices for seven, three for nine, and five for eighteen and things like that. So you had to wait a wee while till, not quite dead man's shoes, but till somebody graduated, and when somebody graduated and got out, then they were able to take on another apprentice, or if they were taking on two or three more men, they were allowed to take on another apprentice. So it was very, very strictly controlled, and the printing trade was very strong in those days, very strong.

Well, once you in actual fact passed the exam, they took you in to work in the office — I was a message boy in the mailroom, just delivering messages. And there was three of us at the time, always. There used to be three young boys and you were in what they called 'The Hall', and you were the 'gofers' for everybody. They weren't called 'gofers' in those days, but you were the 'gofer' for everybody. Distribute the mail when it came in in the morning, once the postroom had sorted it all out, and then you were there during the day just to go messages for anybody and all body. My first wage was nineteen shillings and eleven pence. They didn't give you a pound. They gave you nineteen shillings and eleven pence. I could never understand that. I think I must have been in The Hall about ten weeks and then I got my time started in the letterpress machine room.

My apprenticeship was seven years, but in actual fact you got a year off for doing National Service. National Service started at eighteen, but depending where you were with your exams at night school and the day school, if you were going to be nineteen when you were finishing it, you were allowed a year's exemption so that I didn't go to the Air Force until I was nineteen. I should have gone at eighteen but didn't for the simple reason I was sitting printer's exams in those days, what they called City and Guilds Certificates, which I suppose is the equivalent to Higher National now or SVQs. But in those days, they were very highly rated and they always insisted that, well, they didn't insist but they really liked their apprentices to go in for all this. There were four grades. There was Intermediate, Final, Qualifying and Full Tech, and it was a six-year study course. And it wasn't modules in those days either, it was just a six-year study course plus of course you did have to go to night school over and above that and the night school was just for basic English and for some printing theory. Then there was a day-release class to go to the Heriot-Watt once a week and that was a three-year course. And the printing department was in the Cowgate, where the new Sheriff Court building is now.

You had to wait a year, just to see if you fitted in before they actually sent you to the Watt. You were a second-year apprentice if my memory serves me right before you actually went to dayschool. I was quite interested and quite keen and I went back at night for night classes as well in all sorts of things. So I got up to City and Guilds Certificate. When I got all my certificates I said, 'Look here, I don't want to be stuck on a machine all the time. I've studied all these times.' And management told me quite frankly, 'It's not the policy of Nelsons to promote technical staff onto the administration', what we called admin side, but it was what you'd call blue collar and white collar, I suppose. It wasn't the policy to promote blue collar workers onto white collar jobs, and as such if you were going to get a white collar job, it would have to be as a manager in your own department or something like that, which was really, *really*, *really* dead man's shoes! You could wait thirty or forty years for that kind of thing, you see! And so, at that stage I said, 'Well, if that's the policy and that's it, I'm not going to waste all my time here,' so I went and moved to an Aberdeen paper mill and did some technical work for them. I was thirty years with them after I left Nelsons. So I was twelve years in Nelsons, six as an apprentice and six as a full-time journeyman.

The first year's training as an apprentice was really just watching somebody doing something. You sat beside a journeyman and you just watched what he did for the first six, nine months. You helped him with some heavy lifting. But in the main you were just going along for the first six or seven months watching him. We also had, in the letterpress department, a series of graduated printing machines. We had a little platen thing, and then we had a little Wharfedale in the corner, two very small machines, and then you moved up to the next Wharfedale before you got onto what they called the Miehle machines, the big Miehles, and after that you could move onto the perfector. There were seventeen machines in the printing department. Seventeen machines and I would have thought it was the size of a good size gym now, you know, a big gym? We had an ink store and we had a paper store further away, and when you wanted paper it just came to the back of your machine when you wanted it and all the printer was there to do was just to make sure the stuff was printed.

So there was a range of machines all the way along and after six months, when an apprentice who was on the platen machine moved on, you got to do the work on the platen. And that included business cards for the reps, letterheadings, just the jobbing work that you would do in a jobbing printer's. And we used to do all our own inhouse printing, and after six months, you were the apprentice in charge of all that. The gaffer or the foreman always came along and kept an eye on you. Once you did about six or nine months on the platen and the next apprentice was coming into the system, you moved onto a little Wharfedale which in those days, I think it was the double demy size machine.

And so as a young apprentice after your first six, nine months, you got onto this machine. And suddenly you were also doing other more important work. If they had printed a whole book somewhere else and they had found a mistake in one of the plates or on two of the plates, it was either bashed or damaged. Something had gone in and there was a cut across the plate and the wording was off-centre, and then when they got to the stage of the bookbinding session, it was like, 'Well, look at that!' But what they would do is they would print four pages on this little machine, and take these offending four pages out and then stitch them into the inside of the book so that it was there for corrections. And then from there you graduated up into the bigger machines, and into thirty-two page work on the machines.

Once you got to your third and fourth year, you were considered proficient enough to work your own machine and learn on your own and do your own work with occasional help from the foreman. By the time you got to your fourth and fifth year, you were doing journeymen's work, for an apprentice wage. Although there was not the same pressure on you to produce the work in the time that the journeymen were doing it, but of course you being a laddie, you said, 'I'm going to keep up with this bugger!' You know, and you did it in exactly the same time as the men. But of course, at that time, you were nineteen, twenty, you were a man in all other facets, so you were saying, 'If he's doing it at thirty, then I can do the same job at nineteen, twenty,' and you kept up with them. So there was that side of things as well. There was no pressure put on you by management to keep up with the Joneses but they knew damn fine you would! Because no boy would want to be seen to be slow — and therefore you got more responsibility and more responsibility until, as I say, your last two years of your apprenticeship, you were doing fully-fledged journeymen's work.

And then Nelsons had a whole battery of rotary presses in a slightly different letterpress department just away from the main flatbed area, and that was very much regarded as second-class work. It was very rough and ready down there. But you had to go down there for a year of your time, so it was a broadening of your education as well to work in the rotary department. The impression was in the place that they never put the most highly-skilled printers down in the rotary department. The ones with the craft skills were always on the flatbed side, whereas the rotary lads were just churning it out. I suppose it was equivalent to the newspapers in those days — we felt there wasn't the same degree of required skill to be a rotary printer as to be a flatbed printer.

The Nelson dictionary was done on the rotary thing, mainly because I don't think they'd have revised it ever all the time I was there. And the *Nelson's School Dictionary* was a very popular educational thing, and they just used to bring the plates out once every year and run a hundred thousand off on the rotary, print them up, send them out to schools. And then the plates would be put away again and next year the plates would come out again and, 'We're doing the Dictionary again, lads', and that was it. There was a fair bit of that kind of just run-of-the-mill work, if you know what I mean. But upstairs in the flatbed department you tended to get the pick of the work, or the work that required a bit more skill. The rotary end was the lower end of our achievements, if you like, or the work skills. And yet we had six rotary machines and they churned the stuff out. They were much faster, but there again, as I say, they weren't needed to be anything other than just the workhorses.

Nelsons had a set system of books, the dictionaries, Teaching in English Series, educational books, children's books, and Classics, the Dickens classics, *Nicholas Nickleby*, all that kind of stuff. There was never any pressure on them to keep up with the Joneses, keep up with new machinery. Occasionally we would get new books to print, a new author. Like one by David Howarth called *The Shetland Bus*, which is a very famous book. It was a little tug thing that used to go between Norway and Shetlands with spies during the war. That was a very big seller for them. And we've reprinted that three or four times on the basis that it was a bestseller. We were the first people to publish it.

Nelsons in those days was very famous for a book called *Royal Crown Copy*, which was the initial book for youngsters in primary schools to learn to write. And the top line was the word and the next line was a blank and you had to copy that into the next line and then the next line. And they sold millions and millions of these all over the world! It was called *Royal Crown Copybooks*, they must have had the copyright for this over many years there. And it was the standard way of teaching five, six, seven-year olds how to do joined-up writing. And although they were printed, they had to have a kind of a semi-thick cardboard cover on the thing, much as you would have on a paperback nowadays. And these were printed on this Wharfedale machine. And it wasn't a terribly exciting job, but at least you were bookprinting, and you felt top of the world 'cause you were part of a book that was being printed and going out all over the world at that time. And of course, you were now a year old in the trade and you were a real printer! And we used to have to print these, I mean there were millions of them! And it was always done in a metallic blue ink which got everywhere. As a young laddie, of course, the ink went everywhere and you used to come home with this metallic blue ink all over you, and your mother used to say, 'Oh, get into the bath there, and get out that, get that ink off you.' But it was one of Nelsons staple products in those days.

Some of the most popular work that Nelsons printed was

Thomas Nelson and Sons

called the TES series. They used to do a lot of educational
books, and this was the Teaching in English Series. And
everybody used to say, 'Oh, not TES again,' because it was
straightforward but quite boring to do the actual work. We
had a very good rotary printing department that produced
most of that TES book stuff. And there was the old Classics.
the Dickens Classics, the Shakespeare Classics, the Brönte
Classics. It was done on fairly thin paper, thicker than Bible
paper but fairly thin paper and that was a very good runner
for Nelsons in those days. They used to do thousands of
those, again, for educational purposes, schools and that
kind o' thing. In those days, of course, you didn't share a
Dickens book between three of you, you got one each at
school.

One of the other things when I was in at Nelsons originally
was that the Oxford University Press, their licence expired for
printing the Bible, in the '50s. And every company kind of
jumped onto the bandwagon then. There was Good News
Bibles, Commentaries, Catholic commentaries and many
others. And Nelsons jumped into that too, in a big way.
And they started printing all sorts of commentaries, Good
News Bibles, and modern translations and this kind of thing.
And we did a lot of that work as well. The difficulty with that
was it was very light paper, what they call Bible paper, ten
double crown paper, and it's so thin that, well you know
what the Bible thickness is. And you couldn't run the machines very fast because as soon as you did — Phew! The
paper just went all over the place! And you had to run the
machines very very slowly and even then, there was all sorts
of problems with it. There was also great difficulty in getting
it printing the register back-to-front at the right time and
making sure they were right. Normally if you looked at a
book there used to be a headline on a book and you would see
the one heading backing onto the other — that was terribly
difficult. The Nelsons machines were not the most modern

94

for doing that kind of work and we had a lot of problems working with old machinery.

Occasionally a big run for us would be fifty or seventy-five thousand copies. That would be a very big run for us. Normally, our run would be between ten and twenty-five thousand copies of a book. That would be a normal run for us. But if we were doing fifty thousand or a hundred thousand, that would be exceptional. I can't think of an occasion we'd have many more than that. And then books of birds and cacti, these were specialised runs of four to five thousand at a time. But they were so specialised. They did have what I would call, or what I would now recognise as a niche market. And they just plodded along doing all this stuff in the niche market. I'm sure they made money in those days. It went so well. I think pre-war they were probably a much more prestigious company than that. I think we lived on the reputation quite a bit in the '50s and the '60s.

We had a very good connection with James Brown, the papermakers at Penicuik, and they supplied a lot of our stuff, but we regarded that as quite poor material that they produced. I don't know what the relationship was, but they supplied us with a lot of paper. We worked with a complete range of paper, from the thin what they called India paper. Ten double crown. And you worked up to that thick almost blotting paper style for children's books. So you went through the whole range, to art paper as well, if you were doing some of the good quality printing work as well. I wouldn't like you to think that Nelsons produced rubbish. Well, they didn't. In actual fact they could produce quality printing when required.

One of the other main sellers at that time was kiddies' books. And that was all done on thick paper, what we called an antique wove, which was a very heavy paper, for kids' use. It was loose fibres, really loose fibres. It wasn't knitted together properly and the fibres were all over the place.

And I don't understand how we didn't have the equivalent of asbestosis, 'cause it was so thick and flying around and no masks or anything were available. But I suppose paper being a soluble substance, it just disappeared when it got into your body stream and you just melted it away, passed it away, whereas asbestosis you can't. So when it got into your lungs, I suppose you just washed it away, being fibrous material.

But of course, that was a very cheap paper, and the mere fact that it was cheap meant you had a lot of dust on it, and you just couldn't keep the machines clean with the fibres coming off the paper and you were continually what they called 'washing up'. In other words, after twenty minutes the middles of the E's would fill in, you know. A an' O would fill in somewhere because there would be a fibre in it or something like that and you just couldn't stop and pick it out all the time, and every twenty minutes you had to stop and wash all the ink off the machine, wash all the plates in it, wash everything all again, and start all over again. It was a time-consuming process plus of course you were filthy and got muck over you.

The work that people liked was artwork, when you knew you were working with art paper. It was expensive so you were expected to produce an expensive job, which meant that you could take your time in doing it. So there wasn't the same pressure on you to produce the stuff quickly and you got more time to do it. That was the prestigious work. But again, that was something else that Nelsons persevered with in terms of good sellers for them. They were also quite famous for printing good ornithology books, or books of a very high standard. Ronnie Nelson himself, young Nelson as he was known, was a railway buff. He was the original railway anorak, I would have thought! And what he was interested in, funnily enough, was Swiss railways, mountain railways in Switzerland. And he would get commissions for this all over the world. And we used to have to print photographs of Swiss trains going up and down the mountain. Plus ornithology books on British birds, where it was a four-colour print on the one side, or five-colour print on the one side, beautiful illustration of a bird, the kind of thing *The Reader's Digest* does quite well now. We were doing them, I would say in the '40s and '50s. And on the other side was a type, just typeface, and it was on artwork paper, very glossy artwork paper. And these books, in those days in the '50s, sold for two and three guineas at a time equivalent to fifty pound now, that kind of thing, but in the '50s, they were two and three guinea books. And we had quite a reputation for printing that kind of book as well.

So we had a wide range of printing in the letterpress department and the job was very varied. It was also a family atmosphere in the place. We had a family atmosphere long before the Japanese invented it. Ah, we were a very close-knit group. Very seldom did people leave and go somewhere else. If someone went somewhere else for another job, it was quite a major scandal, not a scandal, but people raised their eyebrows. If you suddenly said, 'I'm chucking it. I'm going to Constables[1] or I'm going to Clarks'[2] or something like that. I suspect at that time that most printers were paid exactly the same. Apart from the newspapers. These boys always got more money because of the unsocial hours and that kind of thing. But in the main, firms like Constables, Clarks, and the big book printers (Morrison & Gibb was the big book printers in the town in those days), the wages must have been very similar. And so that's why there was never much movement.

One of the famous things that Nelsons had at one time was a thing called the Nelson Bed. Now, normally the stereotype plates were on a honeycomb bed with clips on either end and you adjusted it. The Nelson Bed was slightly different in that they were only held on the two oblong lengths. And there was nothing holding it sideways whereas in the honeycomb bed, they were gripped all round and they couldn't move. The problem with the Nelson Bed is that even if you gripped it tight that way, with the constant friction on it, sometimes the plates moved laterally sideways. And that created a little problem with it. But it was a very famous thing and no other printer ever took it up, mainly because it was very heavy. It really was made of cast steel and it did slow the machine down: there was a lot of extra power needed. Although it was very quick to assemble your plates on the Nelson Bed. But it was never a success other than for Nelsons. We used it all the time instead of wooden blocks. Some firms used to have a wooden block and put the plate on the top and tack them down to that. Others had this honeycomb bed. Others printed straight from type in a form. We never had that. We always printed from plates, electro-plates or nickel plates and stereo-plates or straight onto this Nelson Bed, and we were quite famous for it. A lot o' them, other firms, used to turn their nose up at this — a 'We're superior to that' kind a' thing — but it worked very well for Nelsons and it was a very quick process of working.

In the morning, you would go up to the chap and he would say, 'Right, your job today is sixty-four pages.' Thirty-two pages was two signatures, a signature being sixteen pages. So you would put thirty-two pages on this Nelson Bed and you were allowed about five and a half or six hours to get it ready for print. You ensured all the print was even, all the ink was even and everything was right, the position on the paper and all that, and then you used to run it. And we used to run the machines at round about five hundred sheets an hour, depending on the kind of paper you were running and depending on what you were doing. If there was a ten thousand run on the job then you would just run that job off and then you would get the other thirty-two pages which backed onto the first thirty-two. In other words, you were doing two, four, six, eight, ten, twelve on the one side, and then you were doing one, three, five, seven, nine on the other side. So what you did was you printed the sheet and then they turned the sheet over and while the labourers were turning the sheet over, you were getting the second side ready. I can't remember what the system was for the signatures and things but it all worked out and then you went to the proofreader. He checked it. There was a certain way of folding the whole sheet up and he would cut it once you sorted it and then he would just flick through to make sure one was backing on two and three was backing on four and that kind of thing. It was all checked then put through.

All the time I was in Nelsons, twelve years in the printing department, we only had three new machines. Most of the machines that were there were in use twenty years before I went and were still running. In the twelve years I was there, we only bought three new machines. One was a perfector which printed both sides of the sheet at the one time. And the other two were quite fast-running machines. Whereas normally we would run at five hundred an hour, these two machines were capable of running at three thousand an hour. We never had them up to that speed, mind, but they were capable of running at that speed. And they did a lot of work and they just speeded everything up. But Nelsons were never great modernisers. They were never at the forefront of technology. When photo-composition came in they didn't bother with that. The cameras were the old ones with the hood over the top and — they didn't have magnesium flares, but they had everything else, I think. And they never ever altered all the years we were there in terms of modernising the plant. The Monotype keyboard side was making lines of type and monotype up. But the machines were very old and they cluttered and cluttered and cluttered and cluttered. It was just like a weaving machine with the bobbins going back and front with this clutter, clutter. And yet they had the chance to do a lot of photo-composition but it was only at the very end that they did get one or two in to do that. They were never at the forefront of technology.

In the process department, when we were doing special jobs, the type was so poor, we had to sharpen a piece of wood, put printing ink on it and fill in, with a magnifying glass, the holes in the type, you know, and then that was photographed onto a litho plate so that it was right. The stuff was so old at times, it's just not true. They just worked on and on and on with it. And they got away with it for so many years at Nelsons. I think some of the others like T. & A. Constables, Morrison & Gibbs and R. & R. Clarks, they were much more prone to look at new machinery and new methods of doing things than Nelsons ever were.

I can name all the lads who were running the machines right along the back of the room. Hastie, who was an overtime fanatic. Hastie the Dabber, and dabbin' was a slang word for overtime. Hastie would take every hour of overtime going that he could. And then when things got quieter again a bit, and you'd think, 'Do you think we're working overtime next weekend?', and sure as fate, he would come back, 'Yeah, we're over, we're doing over.' He would spear all the information out. So there was Hastie. Next to him there was Drummond. And next to him there was Jock the Horse. And next to him there was Bertie Horne. And then when Jock the Horse got moved, I got moved into the back row in there. And there was a chap called Mercer, and MacMillan who did the big Huber perfectors, and Mercer was very, very posh, he was the only one in the place that read *The Scotsman* and the *Bulletin*. And then there was Alex MacMillan, who was our equivalent to a spiv. He could get anything! Butcher meat, or anything! The boss only needed to say, 'I need sausages', or butcher meat or something, and MacMillan would bring it in the next day. He was always getting stuff that fell off the back of a lorry. And then there was Charlie Hamilton. There was Hamilton, Urquhart and old Jock Muir, and their combined ages must have been about two hundred! Between the three of them on that row of machines. And then there was Moxie, Jock Murray, and Jock Murray married a health visitor or nurse, very posh. He married late in life. He stayed up Spring Valley Gardens. He didn't like anybody to know he worked in a factory, so he used to come in with a belted raincoat and kid gloves every day and collar and tie, sit right down, put his overalls on, do his work, and then go home at night. He had always kid gloves on, the belted raincoat, collar and tie. I don't know what the people in the street thought he worked at, but some kind of obviously an executive job. He had everything except a briefcase with him, if you know what I mean. And Jock Murray, he always had a wee tiff about himself and things. And he worked with a bloke called Moxie who used to stay in Milton Street. And Bert was very much, 'A spade's a spade'. And then there was the young apprentices. And then there was Irvine Kelly, who came on to the new machine and nicknamed Irvine the Budgie.

There was people like Jimmy Muir, and old Muiry, he was in his seventies. Charlie Hamilton was sixty-eight or sixty-nine. No, people didn't think of retiring. I have something in my mind that says that the life expectancy in those days was short, not as many pensioners. You know, I suppose sixty-five was life expectancy. I have recollection of a lot of people dying in the place and that may seem macabre, but people died before they actually finished work. We never had retirement parties and we never, we never seemed to have people saying, 'Well, I'm away.' Oh, there was always one or two who went at 65, but no, I'm sure that there were people who stayed on after sixty-five.

People were just entitled to work and you just let them work on if they wanted to work on. Of course, it was full employment, I suppose, but it was hard enough to get into the printing trade in the first instance, I mean you really thought you'd achieved something getting in the printing trade as opposed to painters. I don't suppose anybody looked forward to retire — No. People did work on after sixty-five. Maybe that's why I've got a recollection of people dying in harness, you know, being carried out the place and things, or going home on the Friday and no' coming on the Monday and they was deid over the weekend or something, he'd died over the weekend. I have a, yeah, I have quite a recollection of that.

Everybody had a nickname. Jock the Horse and Dabber Hastie and Murray and the whole lot of them had them, Smiler, Kelly the Budgie. Kelly got Kelly the Budgie for the simple reason he come in one day and he says, 'I'm awfully depressed.' 'Oh, what's wrong?' 'The budgie died at the weekend.' And everybody just looked at him. There's got to be a punchline here, a joke, you know. And he was so serious! And his budgie had died at the weekend. I still remember thinking, I can't believe this, I really can't believe it! So after that he got Kelly the Budgie, 'My budgie's deid!' And he had a wee squeaky voice. So he got, as I say, after that he got Kelly the Budgie.

Jack McMillan was called Mallom for some reason, and Jock the Horse. Yes, there was a lot of that kind of thing in the area, in the department and things, you know. A lot of fun as well, you know. They were always playing little practical jokes on one another and they were playing practical jokes on the apprentices as well. There was a fair bit of that and you used to get a lot of wrangling about your rites of passage and things and growing up and that kind of thing.

If we were talking about a hierarchy and a structure in printing, I suppose you could say top, lithographers, compositors, printers and then binders. That was how people viewed the thing, you know. Everybody thought they were superior. Process workers thought they were by far a superior trade to the rest and they looked down on compositors and printers and stereotypers (I don't know if it was a class thing or not) but they always came in suits and they just put overjackets on. We couldn't put overjackets on because of the flying machinery. We had to put on boilersuits in those days. But even then, the printers never went home in their boilersuits. They always took them off and dressed and went outside in the main street and you couldn't tell whether he was coming from the office or whether he was coming from the factory floor. They had a bit of a tiff about themselves in the printing trade.

I think binders didn't get as much money as printers. I think their wages were slightly lower. There was more of them too, and a lot of their work, unless they were doing case-making which is making the cases for the actual books, a lot of their work was fairly manual. The stitching and things like that was pretty manual work, although it was a trade and a craft.

And there were a lot more girls in the bindery as opposed to the other departments. There was no girls in the compositors' department, at all. No girls. No girls in the process department. So I think we just equated the fact that more women in the place, then the less skilled it was, if you know what I mean? It was like the whisky bond next door, all the women working in the bond, it wasn't a skilled job, so therefore you equated lack of skill with the amount of women in the place. And so I suppose that had something to do with it as well in the way people thought about things.

Everybody had — until automatic feeders came along — a girl called a layer-on, and it was her job to take a pile of sheets at the back and just push them into the machine one at a time, and that's all she did all day, you know. Just pushed one sheet at a time into the machine, and then the grippers caught it, took it around and printed the sheet and then it came out the other end, and you were watching as it came out the other end. There was a gang of them, I would guess about sixteen of them in the department, and they used to sit in the corner and when you needed one, you just went across and whistled. Oh, nothing like women's lib in those days, just (whistles), 'Over here!'. And you whistled on one and they come running and they worked away with you. And then, after they had printed five hundred sheets, they used to come down and sit on a stool at the end of the machine and you would have to go and lift another ream up, five hundred sheets, sort them out a bit, and then say, 'Right, let's go again,' and we'd start away again. And that's what they did all day.

There was a mixture of age. There was about three or four seniors who were, I suppose when I was fifteen, sixteen, what I would call old, but they were probably forties and fifties. And then there was one or two girls in their teens and twenties, and very seldom in between ages, twenties, thirties, forty. The occasional spinster or something who just come along. But no, they were still there because they were still doing manual feeding into the machines.

They had a little corner which was an alcove. And they could make their tea in there and sit and do their knitting while they were waiting to be called out again. They just sat in that small group until they were called on to do some work. In the main they got on very well together. There was never very many stramashes between the girls. Occasionally, they didn't speak to one another for a couple of days. Just the same as you got a couple of men not speaking to one another for two or three days. But it never really lasted for any length of time. Occasionally, there was a spat between a layer-on and a printer, who criticised her work or something like that, or criticised something about her. And they didn't speak for some time. Now that went a wee bit longer. Couldn't speak for a fortnight or three weeks. But what happened there was that when you came in and it was her turn to come out, she wasnae speaking to him. So somebody else would come and work with you, if you had a ramsammy with one of the other girls and it was her turn 'cause although you had your own girl on your own machine, they did take it in turns as well, you know. 'I've just come off a machine, so I'm due a sit still', and one who hadn't been out for an hour and a half went out and did the next job. And there was always a, 'So who's next for the layer on', you know. And if it was somebody who you didn't really want to do the job for you, you used to hang about till somebody else got her and then you went in for your own one. There was always a jockeying for positions and jockeying for the right girl.

Some of them had a touch. There used to be two front guides and a side guide like an L-shape, and depending on how smoothly they put it into the guides, depending on how, when the guides lifted and the grippers caught it, how well that sheet printed on the back of the other sheet and register. And of course they used to blame you for not having the grippers set right and not having the guidelines set, and there was always little stramashes about that kind of thing. But yes, there was some girls who had a touch, and other girls who were bloody hash-bashy, just the same as those men who had a light touch for doing things and other men who were pretty hash-bashy, you know. So there was sometimes differences in the quality of the people who did the laying on.

But then again, you used to try to work it that you got your favourite one with you or someone that you got on with and was capable of doing the job. There were some girls who were better at it than others. And there were some who were pleasant and enthusiastic and there were some grumpy, so you obviously didn't want a grumpy one if you could avoid it, or if they were in a bad mood, and you wanted somebody you could talk to for a second or two that was pleasant and you could joke with. A fair bit of sexual innuendoes, innuendoes that you would *never* get away with nowadays! Never ever, but it was just common, as a garden everyday language in those days. Perceptions have changed so much, and people's attitudes to each other have changed so much.

If they were putting some new machine in, they would put

an automatic feeder in and get rid of a girl. And certainly towards the last three or four, the last five or six years probably, new machinery was all automatic feeders, lifting the paper and putting it in one at a time and so getting rid of a wage, that kind of thing. But even when I left, there was still girls left. They got married and families and there was no such thing as pregnancy leave and all that kind of thing, you know. You just left, you got married and the kids come along and you stayed at home and looked after the kids. You didn't come back to work in those days. So there was natural wastage there. But at no time was there nobody in the department. There was always girls around, same with the bindery I think.

The dilutees started in the '50s.[3] That was pressure from the Master Printers Association. If you wanted another couple of pound on your wages, you'll have to take people in and train them up as printers within two years. And that really became the end of the actual mystique about being a craftsman. We took them. They were looked down on, obviously, by not having served any time or anything like that. And they were given the most menial of printing jobs to do.

One of the things that Nelsons used to do a lot was what they called 'Bible wall pictures', a picture of about two feet wide and three and a half foot long. It was scenes depicted in the Bible for use in Sunday schools, Moses parting the Red Sea, and Jesus at the water, or the Sermon on the Mount and all that kind of thing. And that was done on machines and printed as a five-colour job. But what they couldn't print at the time was the title of the picture across the bottom, that had to be run through separately. Like, 'Jesus Casting the Net', or 'Jesus Walking on the Water', or 'The Burning Bush', or 'Moses and the Burning Bush'. And this had to be printed separately. And that's the kind of job the dilutees got, to run the printing through at the bottom of the picture. And it was an extra on-cost on to the job. But there again, when they came in they were never ever really accepted. They were accepted as people. They were looked down on in terms of, 'Well, you're not really printers, are you?' There was a sort of cachet about being a printer and serving six, seven years of your time.

The unions were forced to take them on but there was a compromise about one to every twelve or fifteen printers or something like that. There wasn't a flood of them. They were still there when I left. I don't know whether they changed their status or something in the fact that they'd been there all this time. They came in and watched and they were supervised a bit into, 'Right, that's the job, that's it running, if anything goes wrong, come and tell me' kind of thing.

The bosses in charge, the real boss in charge of the place was the Works Manager and at the time we were there it was a chap, a fair bit o' the time, called Hogg, who came in from the outside supposedly to shake the place up, but he soon fell into the ways of the place. And it was a kind of sleepy medieval — I mean, when you see how some companies — when you see the way some other businesses run, you realise that Nelsons perhaps was (medieval's the wrong word) but there was a sort of a, laissez-faire kind of 'Yes, the job will get done, but don't actually treat it with a lot of urgency'.

It was a very placid place in many ways. It certainly wasn't a militant place in any shape or form. But mind you, we had some terrible bosses! I mean, real old school stuff. If the two of you were passing and you stood and talked in the middle of the floor, and if you uttered more than three sentences, then he had sort of what we called the OP, the observation post, it was just a little office in the middle, with the glass all round and he just used to [knocks], 'Get on with your work!' And you couldn't even stop to talk to people, and if you talked more than two or three minutes, he was down on you like a ton of bricks or glaring at you.

And woe betide you if you turned your machine off at five to five. You should run your printing machine until about two minutes to five and you had two minutes to clean everything up, clean up and then go for your coat. You couldn't turn the machine off at five to five because that would have meant you had two minutes spare between four fifty-eight and five o'clock where you were hanging around doing nothing. So you had to run your machine right up to the very end and they were quite strict about that kind of thing. Same with starting up in the morning, at half seven or eight o'clock whenever you started up, they expected to hear the first machine running about three minutes past eight. We used to stand around three or four of you in a group in the corner and just chat about the previous night's, well the radio I suppose it would be, it wouldn't be television in those days, the radio or weekend football. And then the foreman used to come along and say, 'Right lads, let's have you!' And as soon as he said, 'Let's have you!' you just disappeared and went straight to your machine and worked away. They used to watch you, and at five past eight if you weren't running your machine, the boss would come across and say, 'Got a problem?' They were very strict that they got their pound of flesh in terms of you had to have your machine up and running and ready to go when you were printing something at that stage.

Very strict! And as for the apprentices it was a very rigid system in learning and behaviour, but there was always ways of getting around it. For instance, you weren't allowed to make tea because the Misses Parks provided tea, but they used to make the tea at quarter past eight and just keep it boiling till ten o'clock. And you can imagine what that's like! Stewed tea. So the boys thought, to hell with this! So those of us who were a little bit adventurous in those days, we got the little billy can — a big syrup tin and you put the wire through it and put in on a Bunsen burner of some kind, and boiled up your own. But the boss of course knew this was going on and used to try and catch you, so we used to go into this little room to do it, and there was a hole in the door. And one stood guard while the other one boiled the hot water, you see? And I remember this day a chap called Bob Moxie, he was looking after the tea, and he was standing there and I was looking through the door and I says, 'He's coming, Bob!' and Bob picked up the billy can but the wire had fallen down onto the flames and it was red-hot, the wire. And he just said, 'Ph' — He'd just about severed his fingers with this wire going right through his fingers! There was kind a' funny things like that always went on. Being young apprentices and being daft in those days, we had a map on the wall and it divided the room into sections. It was a huge room. And wherever the boss was, we stuck a flag in that area, so at any given time during the day, you could see this flag and find out just exactly where Willie Graham was. And if he was away at that far corner, you had two or three minutes to at least do whatever you wanted to do without being shouted and bawled at. So we had all these kinds of systems amongst the apprentices in the one corner.

A chap called Willie Milton eventually became Secretary of the union, the trade union movement. Willie was, I don't know what you could call him. He was slightly to the left of Willie Gallacher, I suppose, or Mannie Shinwell. And he couldn't see anything good in the bosses at all, and there was always suspicion if the bosses suggested anything. Most of us went along with it because we paid our money. We knew we had to be in the union. The culture was in those days, them and us. That was the culture of the day. So you said, well, unity is strength and we're part of the union, and if it came to us all being together, yes we would. There was never a sort of a proactive thing in the union stuff that we were doing, you know. We responded to certain situations but I couldn't actually say that we initiated any troublemaking of any kind, you know. We were quite happy just to let things slide along and that. Even the strike, when it happened, I think we were dragged into it rather than we rushed into it. Alright, when it happened we were solid enough with it. There was no blacklegging and nobody ever broke the strike, you know. A couple might have wanted to, but you never did that kind of thing in those days. You never walked past a picket line, you were very much sheepishly led. Anything for a quiet life. Nobody wanted to rock the boat. The union, although it was there and although we had union meetings, Father of the Chapel called a meeting about certain things. When there was shift work introduced and all sorts of minor irritations developed, you had a meeting. But I can't ever recall them being terribly militant on anything. Occasionally there was one or two people who were militant as you will get in any society. But in the main, taking everything as a broad picture, I would have thought that we were non-militant as a group, in the trade unions. I don't even know which were more militant — I have a feeling that the bookbinders were. You know how your miners got the name of being militant, motor workers — comps were not more militant than the rest of us. Mainly, I think, although we were working class, and I hate the word working class, but we were, we were all working class, but we felt we were working class with a modicum of intelligence.

The Father of the Chapel was by rotation. I think we did three months at a time. And of course you could in fact be Father of the Chapel for three months and never have a single thing wrong, no complaints, no nothing, you wouldn't have to go and see the bosses about anything. Equally though, there might be other times when there's a little bit unrest and you were never out the boss's office saying, 'Look, Joe Soap's not happy with this', or 'Why has he been taken off that job and doing something else?' and things like that. And there was never any question of picking the strong Labour or the strong Red for this kind of job. It was democratically done. It's just like your turn to clean the stair. It was your turn to be Father of the Chapel and you got the job of that for three months. It was a set rota and all the printers took their turn. But I can't really recall an awful lot of unrest.

We had one major problem in 1959, which was the big strike. And it was the most wonderful summer you're ever likely to find anywhere, but the lads will tell you this — they couldn't get boys to go on picket, we were off golfing, bowling, fishing and things. It was wonderful! At that time, we got five pound a week strike money and we were earning twelve pound a week, in terms of a wage. Now literally what you were getting was fifty per cent of wages for striking. Can you imagine what that'd pay now? You know, I mean the average wage is what, two twenty, two fifty, a week? Suppose you were getting a hundred and twenty pound a week to go on strike. I mean that was the ratio of the thing. So we weren't bothered ourselves about the strike, in the summertime, it was beautiful weather. But aye, it became very nasty between the Master Printers Federation and the unions. And I always remember, I was quite young at the time, I must have been, what? twenty, twenty-one, just came out o' the services and went back to work. And we had this rally in the Central Halls, Tollcross. It's the sort of thing that the Arthur Scargill miners' strike in the '70s put me in mind of. We went there and this chap gave such a rousing Mein Kampf speech, you know, that at the end of the night, he had us so worked up that, I'm sure if he had said, 'Go out and knock over a couple of tram cars', I'm sure we'd have done it. I can remember coming out of that Central Hall, Tollcross, and I thought, 'Jeez, that really is mob violence', 'cause we were all baying like mad. And I thought, 'What the hell's going on here?' I suppose I was quite impressionable at that age. It was quite frightening, and that's the thing that I remember about union power and strike power at the time. That we will not give in to the bosses, and all this kind of thing. I mean, it really was a them and us situation in that strike. It was a general strike throughout the trade, in Edinburgh. I can't remember if it was Glasgow as well, but certainly Edinburgh, Edinburgh was shut down in the printing trade, completely.

And we went back for very little more. We lost out in the end, after ten weeks we went back to work. I think honour was satisfied on all sides. Everybody came out with credit but what we came out with was overtime for the rest of our natural life! We worked a whole year and a half, every hour that God sent, that we were allowed to work by the unions. On most weeks I worked, well Monday, Wednesday and Thursday, I worked from half seven in the morning till half eight at night. And you were just going home, having a bite to eat, crashing out in bed and you were getting up at half six to go to work at half seven in the morning again. And in the end, this is just a personal anecdote, but in the end, I came out in boils all across my shoulders, right across my back. And the doctor says, 'You're just run down. You've worked far too much.' Wasn't called stress in those days, it was just, you just worked too many hours.

We were getting paid time and a half, you see, because the trade was busy at the time and the backlog the strike created. Sometimes they brought you in on a Saturday morning for extra time but they very seldom brought you in on a Saturday because you got time and a half for Monday to Friday. After twelve o'clock on a Saturday, you got double time. And if you worked on a Sunday, you got treble time. Now in those days, treble time would be, let's see, about twenty-two shillings an hour. And that was a fortune. A real fortune, you know. Our normal wage, I think my first wage as a printer was about eleven pound fifty when my time was out. And that wasn't a bad, that was a good wage.

But going back to this business I was saying that we got half wages for being on strike, every week we paid six shillings and nine pence to the union. This is every week. Now at that time, brickies, plumbers and municipal workers, bus drivers probably were paying, well, two shillings or three shillings but we paid double what anybody else paid, hence the reason our benefits were very much greater. It's a very strong union, used to be it was called the Scottish Typographical Association and there was a National Association of Lithographers and National Association of Stereotypers and we were all in the same boat. We all paid high levies and dues to the union, but equally, the benefits were very much higher.

I lived in Holyrood Road. Practically opposite where the Dynamic Earth is now. So I was ten minutes up the road in the morning for work and then I got married and I lived in the Pleasance. A lot of people lived in the peripheral areas to Nelsons. You either got the bus up from Craigmillar, or you walked to your work. There wasn't an awful lot of people who took buses to their work in those days, and trams. I would have thought less than fifteen per cent of Nelsons people lived outwith the area, and when I say outwith the area, I'm talking about outwith five miles of the area. I would be very surprised if there were more than fifteen per cent, which I'm talking about, say, about a hundred or eighty or ninety out of the six hundred and fifty. Office workers tended to travel further, mainly I think because of nine o'clock start, it was easier for them, you know.

But in the main, a lot of the people lived around Sciennes and Braids, and Gilmour Park and that area. Upper Gray Street and Craigmillar. Drew quite a lot from Craigmillar and the bus came up in the morning from Craigmillar. And again, Lutton Place and Bernard Terrace and Pleasance and that area. Trying to think — out of seventeen printers, the furthest away, or the only one that I can remember was Kelly who lived at Sighthill, and Jock Murray who lived in Morningside, and they would be the two furthest travelled printers out of seventeen. The rest were all within walking distance or got a local bus up from Craigmillar. When you put it like that, it was very much local. You walked to your work in those days, or you got something that was fairly easy on the transport line. You didn't live terribly far from your place of employment. Commuting was not in the vocabulary.

I can remember working Christmas Day for years in Nelsons. Not New Year's Day. And then of course the union fought for that and then Christmas Day and then these kinds of days became national public holidays by general consensus. Christmas wasn't recognised in the same way as it is now, it was just another day. You just went to the watch night service and come home and had your Christmas dinners, wasn't even big. Christmas dinners in those days was steak pies. Turkey was unheard of in the '50s for Christmas dinner. It was always a steak pie for your Christmas dinner. That was a treat, a real treat! So in that sense, Christmas was like very much another working day. It was a Christian festival that we just didn't celebrate.

I think you got the Spring Holiday and the September weekend and you got two weeks at the Trades — you had to take the Trades fortnight which was the first two weeks in July. I think we didn't work on the Friday afternoon of the Trades holidays, or we worked till about three o'clock and then we used to cocoon the machines in dust-wrappers. And that was the only real relaxing time, I think, in the place, where you thought, you don't have to work till five o'clock.

The one thing that created more arguments than anything else, you were allowed 8.02 to clock in. At 8.03, they docked you five minutes, and that was always a real bone o' contention 'cause if you were in the queue and the thing changed when you were at the three, you lost money, although you were in the queue the same length of time as somebody who had clocked in at 8.02, you know. Oh, there used to be *mega*-fights about that.

If there was ten or twelve of you arrived off the same bus at eight o'clock and you lined up in the queue — You had to get a move on, but otherwise, if you were 8.02 you were fine, you got paid your forty hours a week, but if you were 8.03, you got docked five minutes and if you got docked five minutes every day that was half an hour, five fives are twenty-five! So you lost half an hour's pay, for two seconds, in theory. It was always a big bone o' contention in the place and they never ever got that sorted out to my memory. And the rule was that 8.02 was considered okay, and the bosses used to go through the time clocks with a microscope and they knew exactly when and woe betide you if you were a regular, a minute or two late. There was always a fine art about getting in at 7.59. Nobody important wanted to get in at 7.48 or 7.49. You always wanted to be in at 7.59, so there was an art in the time clock situation and the little cards.

And the other stupid thing that they had was that when they paid out the wages, you got it in a little eggcup, with your clock number, time number on it, and you used to line up at five o'clock, very similar to the services, the only thing you didn't do was salute. But you read out your number, '349!' and they looked up to see if 349 was coming forward to take this money out of this little eggcup thing. Now, '350! 351!'

I don't know how they did it, but we struggled to get out the twelve pound, fifty pence, twelve pound fifty, plus or twelve fifty-four — You got a ten pound note, two singles, a fifty, well no, you'd get ten singles, you know. Overtime, you got some fivers in it, but even then it was a hell of a struggle to get this money out the thing, and it was so humiliating. I used to be humiliated, until I went to the services and then it didn't bother you after that 'cause in the services they did exactly the same thing to you. You shouted your number, you went up, you saluted, and you took your money in and went away, but that was in an envelope. But in private life, it seemed to me to be a most degrading experience to go and they hand your money over to you in a little tin cup and you went away, screwed it out and then you looked at it and compared it — because you got your payslip in the morning and then you got the money at night. So you could compare the two. So you knew in the morning what you were going to get at night and then you would wonder about the overtime and all that kind of stuff because that was always hard to calculate, but there was this degrading experience of lining up and the boss shouting your number out, your time card number, and you had to come forward and the clerk handed you the little can. Crazy.

And you were always watching them coming through the door with the tray and at that time you couldn't go and put your coat on before you got your wages and walk out the door. You had to get your wages during working hours and put your coat on after. Oh, very strict protocol, very strict, you know. Whether it was strict or ancient established practice or not, I don't know, but it never ever changed all the time I was there, nobody liked change! Change was dreadful! Oh dear, dear, dear! Can't change anything in the place at all for any reason or anything!

That's another little funny story. One chap determined to impress the boss by reducing what they called the make-ready time — in other words, five, five and a half hours to make a job ready. This chap came in and he started making ready in four and a half hours. Knocking himself out, and of course the boss used him as a carrot for everybody else, or a stick for everybody else! And the poor fellow got the nickname o' Jock the Horse because he in actual fact was really horsed into it and sweated, you know, and he was the most unpopular guy in the place and he was the benchmark for everybody else, but everybody else knew what they were doing, knew that they had five and a half hours to do it. It was sods' law. If you were allowed five and a half hours to do the job, you werenae going to make it ready in three and a half hours. It took your five and a half hours and you just walked away and did the job. The bosses had it calculated out that it was five and a half hours make-ready time so that was properly built into the price and the costing and estimating. Till this lad came along, as I say, who they called Jock the Horse, and he cut it down to three and a half hours and it was, 'Ah well, but he cannae be doing the right job if —'. You know, the usual, he can't be doing the right job, if he's doing it that quick and cutting corners. He caused a lot of friction in the place, and there was always great delight when he messed something up. 'That's what you get for going too fast,' routine, you know!

One of the innovations that happened when I was there near the end was shift work. All of a sudden, about 1957 I would have thought, they introduced six to two, two to ten shifts on machines that were really very busy. And of course there was a hell of a lot of negotiation for what the extra money was for that kind of thing. And then three or four of you were on that shift. So when everybody disappeared at five o'clock, there was only four or six of you in the place till ten o'clock because you started at two and there was a more relaxed atmosphere in there because the bosses were away. There was nobody in. I mean, you still had to do your work because it was in your time sheet and you knew perfectly well the next day your time sheet would be examined. But there was a more relaxed atmosphere, maybe simply because there were fewer of you in the place together, and of course that's when you could make your tea without anybody bothering you. And then, when you did the six to two shift, you were in the hour and a half in the morning before everybody else come in. So again, that was relaxed a bit more. But that was only in certain departments and at certain times when things were busier. But they did introduce shift work into the place, although before that it was very much an eight till five, half seven to five thirty, operation. I'm talking about just after post-war.

People quite liked the six to two shift in the morning 'cause you were up early anyway and you got away at two o'clock and that was you finished for the rest of the day. And like everything else, it had its downside. You changed over on the Wednesday night so you finished at ten o'clock on the Wednesday night but you had to be there for six o'clock the next morning. That's the hardest bit, you know, but then again you got off Friday at two o'clock and you probably weren't in again till two o'clock on a Monday so you maybe had a long weekend to compensate. It's like the American shift systems that a lot of companies are operating now where you work four days for twelve hours and then you have five days off. And a lot of the big paper mills who have continuous production, continuous machinery going, they have that kind of system now of continuous work and you work four days for twelve hours. You knock yourself out but you get five days off, you know. And so that was the forerunner of that kind of thing, on shift work, only because when they were really busy, they wanted stuff out in a hurry and they were prepared to pay for it.

Very little protection was offered. There was the minimum safety guards on the machines. There was a lot of flying bits on the machine that were not covered. There used to be a kind of arm coming forward for delivering sheets. That was on a reel. And twice I got nipped. On one occasion one chap certainly got his tie caught in the grippers and pulled into the machine. The tie material snapped and he pulled his head away. Ah well, fingers, the guillotine boys had always problems with fingers, of course. But I've no real experience of that apart from the apocryphal stories you used to hear about binders walking about with digits missing. Although there were a lot of binders with problems with their fingers. You used to get a lot of checks and crushing of fingers and that. My wedding ring saved me twice. Yeah, there wasn't nearly the attention paid to factory safety in those days. It was very minimal. I never, we never had a serious accident in the place, although you could easy have done with the bed going back and forward over a hole in the ground and that kind of thing. I can't ever recall an ambulance being called to the place for that kind of accident. People took unwell and ambulances came. But, yeah, safety was not a high priority in those days. Maybe it was not a high priority in any job in those days. I don't think we were any different from anybody else. Health and safety at work was not a major issue — again, the Misses Parks, they got the job of being health and safety officers, and they wouldn't know a guard if it hit them in the face. Occasionally, the guillotine boys, they had problems, the cutting and that kind of thing. And they were much more prone to that than printers or compositors and that side of things. So no, accidents and things were not all that prevalent. Oh, a few cuts and things like that, but certainly nothing, I can't recall anything major in all the time, the twelve, thirteen years I was there.

But there was never the emphasis on health and safety that there is nowadays in these kinds of things. A lot of it was taken for granted, and it was taken in the sense that, yes, if something had to be done it was done. If there was a problem with something, then the Father of the Chapel went and said, 'Look here, we're not happy with that, that floor is far too slippy' or something like that, 'You've got to get something done.' Ah, then invariably it was done. Occasionally oil spilt or sections of the place were just not right. A hazard of some kind, and we pointed that out to them. Yes, I'm sure that was done, but without much fuss and things. There was never any consciousness about health and safety, though, as far as I was aware of the place, but maybe that's just time. In relation to nowadays, it was non-existent, in those times. Although they had them, the usual factory notices up, health and safety here and all that kind of thing. It wasn't a problem, or nobody perceived it to be a problem, I would say.

And our canteen was quite good — although we thought it was pretty crappy, rubbishy, it was probably quite to the forefront of works canteens in the '50s and '60s, you know. Soup, meat and veg and a sweet and a coffee, two shillings or something. And the food was very good, it was airy, clean and tidy and there was never any kind of health problems, obviously with the canteens they were all the same, there was something about the sameness about it. But when you hear of the kind of canteens at some of the other places they had, I think we were probably fairly superior in that kind of sense. I would have thought there might have been about a hundred, hundred and twenty used it, out of the work force. A lot of people went home at lunchtime. Those of us who didn't, whose wives were working or doing other things, used it, and yet by the time I left, I had the impression it was probably down to about seventy of us. I put it down to change in social circumstances, but also the fact that there's a sameness about, well, like say going to the same restaurant for year after year after year. If it's Tuesday it must be mince, if it's Friday it must be fish, you know, that kind of thing. And so people would just take sandwiches — plus habits changed as well. People didn't want to eat so much during the day. And we went for a sandwich and a glass, a pint of milk or something, and sat in the park in the sun during the lunch hour. You weren't allowed to stay in the factory during the lunch hour.

In those days, Nelsons had a great social side. I'm talking about right throughout the '50s. In the end, I think it stopped maybe near about '58 or '59 but certainly from the time I went in, you used to go down to Waverley Station and got on board this six or eight coach train, and they would take you across to Rothesay or Dunoon. You would get on one of the paddle steamers in Dunoon, and there was about four or five hundred of us from Nelsons on this train, and you had a day out's picnic. Never cost you a sausage! The Company just paid for everything. But it was the family picnic as it was meant to be, I suppose, in those days. Oh yes, trips 'doon the watter', as they said. In the wintertime, they used to run all sorts of dances in what they called the Institute, which was across the road, which are now houses I think. And that was the canteen. But they used to run dances on a Saturday and there was the two Misses Parks, now when I say Misses, it's M-I-S-S-E-S. There were two sisters, old spinsters and they were the original directors of human resources, welfare officers I suppose. You never called them welfare officers or even personnel officers in those days. But if the girls wanted stuff, you know, for themselves they used to go to 'em and they looked after them. If a girl was having a wee bit o' problem they used to cry on their shoulder and that, the two old dearies. And they actually ran the canteen as well — they were just generally there for the welfare of everybody in the place, you know. Very material.

The lads at the dayschool and nightschool that were my contemporaries and my peer group, you never heard them talk in quite the same way about their employers or how their factory worked. They never had these picnics or Christmas dances that we had, gaddin' kind of thing.

Socially in our days, you went to the Palais for dancing. Ah, no, you went to the Palais for company. You went to the Cavendish Ballroom, which was at Tollcross, for dancing. And you went to the one at Morningside called, I don't know what the hell it's called now — Plaza, that's it, for your education, because that's where all the nurses' hostels were situated in Morningside. So if you managed to go out with a nurse then you knew about the finer things in life! So I mean, you used to say that, as young apprentices, that if you were going to the Plaza or you were going to the Palais, you knew what kind of night you were out for!

Sex was never as open as it is nowadays, but sex played a part in the life of the factory floor, you know, the men and the

women, some of the things the older men said to the girls —
as a young apprentice you were shocked, but some of the
folks used to say things to the girls in there that really just
drew you up, just as a young boy, you know. So there was a
fair bit of — roughness is not the right, well, coarseness is
probably a better word to use. There was a fair bit of
coarseness going on in the place. But then again, maybe that
was just typical factory-floor jargon and banter. And in those
days — I mean, you would get hunted for it nowadays. You
could never say half the things to women nowadays that you
used to say in those days. I mean, the equality of women just
wouldn't stand for it, and it's insulting. The girls never
bothered themselves in those days.

But the point was a lot of these girls married printers or
people in the work, and same with bookbinders. There was a
tremendous amount of that kind of inter-marriage. Marriage,
we used to say marriages weren't made in heaven, they were
made in Nelsons! You know, the amount of couples that have
got married and had families was quite high. I don't know if it
was more prevalent in the printing trade than it was in say, a
plumber's or a builder's or something like that, but it always
seemed to happen a lot.

We had great fun as apprentices. It was a happy place,
working amongst so many girls, and that's all you were
interested in those days, in doing your work and girls and
perhaps getting through night school and passing all your
exams. I mean, your ambitions were limited. Pass your
exams, keep out of trouble, and find out what the opposite
sex was about, and play your sports. What else was there to
life? You weren't interested in anything else, no social con-
sciences or political awareness, that was it. You were con-
tented with your lot in many ways, you know. You wanted to
play for the football team, you wanted to play well, you
wanted to make sure you got to night school and you passed
all the exams so there was no hassle, and you wanted to enjoy

your work. You took pride in your work and you wanted to find out about the opposite sex. End of story!

I suppose it's hard for people to realise now just how important the printing trade was to Edinburgh, and the skills involved in being a printer or a compositor. The same as a watchmaker, I suppose, I mean, that's not putting it on too high a plane, but you know how you admire watchmakers, printers had that kind of aura about them as well, until Murdoch come along with Wapping and all sorts of things that upset the whole applecart and reduced printers to just another job worker.

There was a kind of a folklore about it, in the printing trade, for some reason or other. You were conscious that yes, you were coming into something that was quite special, and that you were not like any other worker. Now, that sounds daft, but that's the impression that the boys in the place gave you. 'You're coming into something different here. You're not just an ordinary worker, son.' 'You learn a skill here, a skill that's valued.' And I think it's 'cause of the tradition in the trade the printers were always regarded as skilled people and the amount of influence that printed word had in the world, as opposed to something else. Cannae get too excited about transistors and capacitors, can you, whereas the book trade, spreading knowledge is probably something that you were always fairly high regarded in — in society and, I'm not saying society, but I'm saying in working class society. If you said what you did, 'Oh, I'm a printer,' then people did sit up and say, 'Oh, that must be an interesting job, and a job of high skill.' You had a kind of cachet, I think's maybe the word, in the circles you moved in, as opposed to some of the others you know which was regarded as construction trades or whatever it was people were doing? It did have a certain amount of cachet about it, I suppose. You always felt that anyway and it was imbued in you by the older printers when you came to work with them in the 'Look here, son, you're not coming in here just to be an ordinary worker, you're going to come in here with some respect and be part of the system.' Certainly from compositors' and printers' point of view, there was that.

Notes

1 T. & A. Constable Ltd, Hopetoun Street, Edinburgh.
2 R. & R. Clark Ltd, Brandon Street, Edinburgh.
3 Diluted labour was substitute labour used in times of labour shortage. Dilutees did not serve an apprenticeship and could undertake only specific tasks.

GLOSSARY

Art paper	Paper coated with china clay and polished to a high finish.
Back	Binding edge of a book.
Back margin	Margin of book nearest the spine.
Bed	Part of a press on which the block, type or plate is fixed, ready for inking and impressing.
Bible paper	Very thin, strong, opaque printing paper used where low bulk or low weight is needed.
Binder	Person who does bindery work.
Bindery	Place where binding is done.
Binding	Process of fastening printed sheets together and securing them in a cover.
Blockmaker	Person who makes a plate for impressing a design or lettering into a book cover.
Bulk	Paper term which describes the degree of thickness of paper.
Camera ready copy	Type or matter or artwork pasted into positioning for photographing.
Case	Stiff board cover of a book. Often covered with cloth, paper or leather.
Case	Partitioned tray containing type for hand composition.
Caseroom	Room with cases of type for composition.
Casting	Process of forcing molten metal into a mould to create a character or slug of type.
Casting machine	Monotype machine or Linotype machine.
Chapel	Smallest unit of a print union's departmental or company grouping.

Clean proof	Printer's proof which has no errors.
Clichagraph	Early form of scanning device.
Cloth binding	Use of cloth to cover the boards of a case-bound book.
Comp	To compose; a compositor.
Compositor	Person who makes up type into lines.
Crown	Standard size of paper (384x504mm).
Dabbing	Overtime.
Demy	Standard size of paper (444x564 mm).
Dilutee	Substitute labour which had not served an apprenticeship.
Display sizes	Size of type larger than 14pt used for display rather than text.
Distribution	Return of letterpress type to the case after printing.
Down time	Non-production time when a printing machine is being maintained or made ready.
Dummy copy	Mock-up of a book or other piece of printing to indicate specifications.
Edition	All the copies of a printed work from the same set of plates.
Electrotype	Duplicate of block or forme made by coating a mould with metal.
em	Width of the body of the lower case m in any typeface. Standard unit of measurement.
en	Half the width of an em. Width of the average type character. Used as the basic unit of measurement for casting off copy.
Father of the Chapel	Elected chairperson of chapel.
Feeder	Mechanism on a press which separates and lifts sheets into the primary position.
Flatbed press	Printing press with flat printing surface.
Folding	Action of folding sheets to make signatures.
Folio	Extra-large book format size; sheet of copy.
Foot	Bottom of a book or page.
Forme	The printing surface imposed and mounted ready for printing.

Glossary

Four-colour process	Colour printing with the three subtractive primary colours (yellow, magenta, cyan) plus black.
Furniture	Letterpress spacing material.
Galley proof	Proof of type matter not made up into page.
Gathering	Assembling the sheets of a book in the right order.
Gutter	Binding margin of a book.
Half-tone	Infinite range of tones of grey between black and white.
Half-tone screen	Glass plate or screen, cross ruled with opaque lines and having transparent squares, which is used to split up the image into half-tone dots.
Head	Top or top margin of a page.
Heriot-Watt	Heriot-Watt Technical College, Edinburgh.
Heriots	George Heriot's School, Lauriston Pace, Edinburgh.
House corrections	Errors introduced by the typesetter which are corrected before proofs are sent to the customer, or marked on the customer's proofs for his attention.
India paper	Very thin opaque rag paper often used for high-quality Bibles. See Bible paper.
Journeyman	Tradesman who has served and completed an apprenticeship.
Keyboard	Array of keys used to input into a system.
Keyboard operator	Person who operates a keyboard.
Lay	Guide on a printing machine which positions a sheet before printing.
Layer-on	Person who guides a sheet for printing.
Laying	Process of feeding paper into a printing press for printing.
Letterpress	Printing from images with a raised surface which impresses on the paper.

Letterpress printer	Person who prints using letterpress method of printing.
Limp binding	Paperback binding.
Linotype machine	Linecasting machine manufactured by Linotype.
Litho	= lithography.
Lithography	Litho printing. Uses principle that oil (grease) and water do not mix. Image is chemically treated to attract greasy litho ink and repel water.
LNER	London and North Eastern Railway.
Matrix case	Case for holding mould from which typeface is cast or photographic master or type fount.
Make-up	Making up typeset material into pages.
Make-ready	The operations involved in preparing a printing machine to run.
Merit money	Additional money paid as merit.
Miehle	Printing press. Also printing-press manufacturer in Germany.
Monotype	Proprietary name of a 'hot metal' typecasting machine which assembles characters individually rather than line-by-line.
Monotype casting machine	= Monotype caster.
Monotype keyboard operator	Person who keys in characters on Monotype machine.
Orphan	First line of a new paragraph or a subhead which appears on its own at the foot of the page. See Widow.
Page make-up	Assembly of the elements in a page into their final design.
Page proof	Proof of a page before printing.
Perfector	Printing press which prints both sides of a sheet at one pass.
Pica system	Unit of typographical measurement equal to 12 points.
Platemaking	Process of making plates for litho printing.

Glossary

Platen	Small letterpress printing machine on which the paper is pressed up against the vertically held type-bed.
Photo-composition	= phototypesetting. Setting type onto a photographic paper or film.
Point system	Main system of typographical measurement.
Press proof	Proof taken from the press after make-ready but before the full run.
Process camera	Camera designed for the various photographic processes involved in printing.
Proof	A trial printed sheet or copy made before the production run for the purpose of checking.
Proof-reader's marks	Symbols used by a proof-reader in marking corrections on proof.
Quoin	A wedge or expanding device used to lock up letterpress chases.
Reader	Person who checks proofs for accuracy.
Reader's proof	First galley proof used by the printer's reader.
Register	Positioning of colours accurately to form a composite image.
Register mark	Marks in same relative position on film or plate to enable correct position to be achieved.
Reprint	Subsequent printing of the first edition of a publication.
Repro	= reproduction Prepress camerawork, scanning and film make-up.
Retouching	Correcting a photographic print or transparency before reproduction.
Rotary press	Printing press which prints from plates on cylinders.
Run	Number of printed copies of a publication.
Scanner	Computer controlled sampling device which reads the relative colour densities of copy and produces colour separations.

Section	A folded sheet forming part of a book.
Signature	Synonym for section, a folded sheet forming part of a book.
Stereotype plate	A duplicate printing plate cast or moulded from a matrix of an extending relief printing surface.
Stone	Surface on which pages of metal type are assembled and planed down.
Tails	Bottom margins of pages.
Typeface	Specifically designed style of type.
Wash-up	Cleaning of the printing units of a press prior to a change of ink or a shut-down of the machine.
Wharfedale	Make of printing press.
Widow	Short cast-line of a paragraph at the top of a page and line of a paragraph on its own at the top of a page. See Orphan.